Praise for Unequal Opportunity...

The Civil Rights Act of 1964 was a federal government response to the denial of economic suppression of certain groups in American society. It was recognized that the adverse treatment suffered by certain groups was so severe that they needed protection. Among the groups covered are race, sex, religion, national origin and color. These groups are known as protected classes. More than forty six years later, Leah Hollis provides us with verification that opportunity in American society continues to be adversely affected by one's protected class membership. The US census indicates that there are more women than men in these United States. Dr. Hollis' work, which centers on current unlawful discrimination suffered by women from diverse backgrounds, suggests that discrimination is not confined to *minority* status. *UNEQUAL OPPORTUNITY* indicates that we still have a great distance to travel on the road to equality.

Kaaba Brunson, Harrisburg Regional Director
Pennsylvania Human Relations Commission

Before discrimination cases become court cases, they are stories, stories of the hopes and dreams of ordinary people, and of how discriminatory behavior in the workplace can cause injury that is deep and profound. In *UNEQUAL OPPORTUNITY,* Leah takes the time to tell the stories of real victims of discrimination, bringing life to the stories behind dull court records in an imaginative and compelling way. This is a book for everyone, from victims of discrimination who want to learn more about options, to employers who want a helpful discussion tool to make the point that, unfortunately, discrimination is still with us and still very real.

Marcella David, Professor of Law and International Studies, Associate Dean for International and Comparative Law, University of Iowa, College of Law

Leah Hollis adroitly depicts the lives of hardworking, educated women who selflessly dedicate themselves to improving the workplace, only to experience the dehumanizing effects of discrimination. Hollis gives new meaning to the old adage, *no good deed goes unpunished*. The heroines featured in **UNEQUAL OPPORTUNITY** are patient fighters who ascend to positions of prominence by embodying grit and determination. Their stories provide inspiration for anyone targeted by discrimination and guidance for employers seeking to avoid costly litigation. The powerful tales of intellectually astute women victimized by arbitrary and capricious employers exposes the unfortunate reality that discrimination is pervasive, even in this era of Barack H. Obama, the first Black President of the United States.

Naomi Ruth Thompson, JD., Associate Director, Office of Institutional Diversity and Equity, Northeastern University

UNEQUAL OPPORTUNITY highlights several incidents of inequality of the nation's invaluable human resource, women power in the workplace. The unspoken violence of injustice stifles productivity of companies and also suppresses talented, creative individuals. As a Diversity Trainer, I use *UNEQUAL OPPORTUNITY* as a guidebook to focus on managing diversity with organizational internal changes. The easy reading guide illustrates that a working environment can be problematic for women. However, it also provides the reader the opportunity to comprehend the magnitude of the inequality and project a possible approach that would generate a diversity-friendly workplace.

Bruce G. Haselrig, Sr., Diversity Trainer
President & CEO- Bruce Haselrig Group

Unequal Opportunity

Fired without cause?
Filing with the EEOC...

Leah P. Hollis, Ed.D.

Library of Congress Control Number: 2013900866

ISBN: 978-0-9884782-3-7

Patricia Berkly LLC is at www.diversitytrainingconsultants.com

Table of Contents

About the Author

DR. LEAH P. HOLLIS, raised in Johnstown, Pennsylvania, is a noted educator, researcher, and lecturer. She has an exemplary career in higher education administration where she has held senior leadership and faculty posts. Dr. Hollis has taught at Northeastern University, the New Jersey Institute of Technology, and Rutgers University. Her work has led her to research this topic on women's experiences in leadership positions. Dr. Hollis received her Bachelor of Arts degree from Rutgers University and her Master of Arts degree from the University of Pittsburgh. She received her Doctorate of Education in Administration, Training and Policy Studies from Boston University, as a Martin Luther King, Jr. Fellow. Also, Dr. Hollis continued her professional training at Harvard University through the Graduate School of Education, Higher Education Management Development Program. She also earned certification in Project Management and Executive Leadership at Stanford University and Cornell University respectively. Further, she has earned certifications in EEO Law/Affirmative Action and Conflict Resolution and Investigation from the American Association for Affirmative Action. Dr. Hollis has served as a diversity trainer for Northeastern University and she speaks regionally and nationally on such topics as race, gender, ethnicity, equality and access.

Acknowledgements

After standing on so many shoulders, I find it hard to itemize and distinguish the countless friends and family who have offered their insight and support in the creation of this book.

It is so true. If it doesn't kill you, it indeed can make you stronger. Thank you everyone.

Thank you to God for lighting the path and providing me with the strength to move forward.

Foreword

Robert E. Gregg, Employment Attorney

EMPLOYMENT can be rewarding and fulfilling. It can also be traumatic. Careers can last a lifetime, end suddenly, or fade with agonizing slowness. Many people have overcome great odds, and devoted years of study, sacrifice and hard work to achieve a career, to then experience the demise of their job. If the end of employment is due to discrimination, the laws provide recourse.

Employment cases are difficult. The legal facts and evidence are not the major difficulty. The litigation process is destructive. Cases take years. By the time one reaches the other end, the original problem is ancient history. In the meantime, the damage only increases with soaring legal fees. The original termination of employment has been personally and economically traumatic. The litigation process can be painful. Once started, it is the rare person who can put their case "on the shelf" and deal with it only when each of multiple strategies of the process becomes active. The process itself can harm one's psyche, marriage, relationship, and physical health. Even if one ultimately wins the case, years later, it is questionable as to whether it was really a "win."

There is, however, an alternative which may bring a quicker resolution, or a measure of vindication. Even better, it is free. The public has already pre-paid with their taxes for this valuable service.

The EEOC has power that no other person can muster. The employer must wake up, take notice and respond! The EEOC can mediate and reach settlements of disputes. It can force an employer to examine decisions on overall practice and make changes. It can make formal findings of "probable cause" of discrimination. Ultimately, it may decide the case is of such significance it may sue on one's behalf and take the case into the courts. Even if the EEOC or state process does not end in a "probable cause," one can feel vindicated. The complainant has not gone meekly and has made a stand! The process has forced an examination of issues, which may cause the employer to think twice the next time, change policies and practices, and create a better environment for others in the immediate future. That is not an insignificant outcome. ONE CAN FEEL PROUD. ONE CAN MOVE ON.

Dr. Leah P. Hollis has compiled a sampling of these situations, and illustrates how several women have used the EEOC and the laws for recourse. This book is about the use and benefits of that EEOC process. Dr. Hollis is an educator and EEO professional who has devoted her life and career to fostering equal opportunity and breaking down employment barriers for all people. *UNEQUAL OPPORTUNITY* tells us compelling stories of others who have beaten the odds, achieved success, then suffered unfair harm, and used the EEOC process for effective resolution. This book leads us into the struggles of people who are in many ways like us. Even though we may not all be of the same gender, race, or orientation of those illustrated in the book, we, too, can understand and feel their dedication, achievements and the harm they endured. We may experience the same, and need this understanding of the available recourse provided by the EEOC and state agencies. This book illustrates the inner workings of EEOC complaints and discrimination cases. They can help one achieve resolution and move on with life and further success.

Fall, 2010

Robert Gregg is an attorney with over 30 years of civil rights and employment law experience. He litigates employment cases and also developed the anti discriminatory policies and procedures for public and private employers throughout the United States. He has authored numerous articles with practical advice on employment practices and presented over 2,000 seminars.

Preface

In 2008, I was chatting with a friend who had been abruptly let go from her job. She was a stellar performer, the quintessential "young, gifted, and black..." She had studied at a private university, was once a stellar musician, and had at least 20 years in the field with several professional certifications. She had spoken internationally in her field, and anticipated ascension to a vice president's position. Given her track record with the series of promotions and raises at her job, she was devastated by an unfair termination initiated by a new boss who felt threatened by her popularity among the staff. As she shared her story with me in hushed tones, in a veil of embarrassment, she also commented that several other colleagues, in different industries and backgrounds, had also faced similar turmoil in their careers. It was a quiet thing people don't often share. Many don't want to admit they were fired, RIF'ed*, let go, or terminated. We so desperately want to believe that the Civil Rights Movement, the Women's Movement, and affirmative action have been successful. *(RIF means reduction in force).

Disbelief fluttered in her heart along with anger, panic, and the voice from her childhood that said, "Don't get new on us- you still BLACK!" But this is the age of African-American presidents, women as Secretary of State, fair housing, and equal pay. What she and I discovered is in the age of the biggest recession since FDR, those in the dominant culture can revert back to a baser self, a self of narcissism and exclusion, rooted in unresolved insecurity.

The FY 2009 data show that private sector job bias complaints (including those filed against state and local governments) which have alleged discrimination based on disability, religion, and/or national origin, hit record highs. While age-based discrimination reached the second highest level to date, the EEOC reported that 36% of its complaints were based on race, 36% were based on retaliation, and 30% were based on sex based discrimination. The near historic levels of filed complaints might indicate greater public access to EEOC information, economic trends, and the increased diversity paradigm changes within personnel ranks; in short, more black and brown people, more people from diverse backgrounds, are educated and in the work force. In FY 2009, the EEOC recouped over $294 million, a record high, through mediations and enforcement that were tied to harassment or charges under the Title VII Civil Rights Act.

During 2009, the number of pregnancy discrimination lawsuits continued to rise. Nationally, 6,196 charges were processed by the EEOC, which was slightly down from 6,285 in 2008, but an increase from the 5,587 cases filed in 2007 and the 4,901 cases filed in 2006. Women are accessing the 1978 Pregnancy Discrimination Act.

In 2010, the EEOC again reported historic numbers in the cases filed. Close to 100,000 new complaints of workplace discrimination were filed with retaliation charges surpassing claims of racial bias. These statistics don't include those who by passed the EEOC and went straight to an attorney to file a law suit.

Inside the volumes of statistics are volumes of personal stories, personal disappointments, and personal consternation. I too had stories of friends, family members, and colleagues who faced these discriminatory practices on the job. Careers were stifled, families broken, houses lost, lives irreparably changed. Even if a settlement came to pass months, even years later, nothing eradicates the stain left on one's heart to hear "you're fired," especially when you know it is driven by discrimination. As I continued my interviews and inquiries, I found women who faced discrimination not only for race, but for religion, pregnancy, sexual orientation, and more. I had to come to terms with the fact that employers discriminate for a variety of reasons, but for the same basic reason, for not being like them.

Readers of this book might react; *no way did all this happen.* These stories are just self-absorbed whiney depictions of victimization blown out of proportion. However, the data demonstrate that not only does this happen, but discriminatory termination happens at alarming rates. While there are many supportive and kind people of all races, nationalities, and ethnicities, all it takes is one racist, sexist or misogynist administrator in an organization to launch this blow, and create havoc for the complainant and defendant. There are no winners once the adverse employment action occurs. There are only hard feelings, poor morale for those employees left in its wake, and potentially a damaged organizational reputation for the employer.

My goal with this book is to present the barbed kernels of EEOC incidents, complaints, and issues, yet couch these real stories in fictional frames to protect the complainants and the integrity of their confidentiality agreements. Some of these stories resulted in settlements, while others simply moved on with the scar of discrimination embossed on their psyche. In all cases, the lives of complainants and defendants were changed forever. These stories are not meant to disparage the wonderful men and women who dedicate their lives to ousting discrimination. Nonetheless, by shining a light on these incidents, perhaps employees can be wary of the warning signs and make strides to protect themselves; and employers, even the unwitting, can see the similarities in themselves and refrain from discriminatory employment practices that hurt all involved. These stories represent a cross-section of the race, age, and gender discrimination that women of all colors face while trying to perform a solid day's work in America. This book is not intended to give legal advice, but is intended to provide insight to trends based on the interviews and stories of women who have endured such hardships.

Please note, as I have utilized qualitative research methods and procedures, I have also taken proper measures to protect the confidentiality of the participants of this study. All information, informed consent documents and interview notes identifying any of the complainants in this book, has been destroyed to protect confidentially and any possible existing nondisclosure statements. Also, as one reads through these cases, the readers might recognize seeming coincidences or similarities to discriminatory scenarios they know. The basic anatomy of discriminatory practice can be similar as the basic motivation for such practice stems from the same basic places. Discrimination in the psyche stems from fear, entitlement and/or exclusion. Thank you to the women who took the time to retell their experiences so others might find the courage and motivation to address similar issues that still face society.

Leah P. Hollis, Ed. D.
2011

Chapter 1

Carrie Roberts—Growing up young, gifted and integrated

The Parable of the Mouse Trap

A mouse looked through the crack in the wall to see the farmer and his wife open a package. "What food might this contain?" the mouse wondered, but he was devastated to discover it was a mousetrap.

Retreating to the farmyard, the mouse proclaimed the warning: "There is a mousetrap in the house! There is a mousetrap in the house!"

The chicken clucked and scratched, raised her head and said: "Mr. Mouse, I can tell this is a grave concern to you, but it is of no consequence to me. I cannot be bothered by it." The mouse turned to the pig and told him: "There is a mousetrap in the house! There is a mousetrap in the house!" The pig sympathized, but said: "I am so very sorry, Mr. Mouse, but there is nothing I can do about it but pray. Be assured you are in my prayers." The mouse turned to the cow and said: "There is a mousetrap in the house! There is a mousetrap in the house!" The cow said: "Wow, Mr. Mouse. I'm sorry for you, but it's no skin off my nose."

So, the mouse returned to the house, head down and dejected, to face the farmer's mousetrap alone.

That night a sound was heard throughout the house — the sound of a mousetrap catching its prey. The farmer's wife rushed to see what was caught, but in the darkness, she didn't see it was a venomous snake whose tail the trap had caught. The snake bit the farmer's wife.

The farmer rushed her to the hospital, and she returned home with a fever. Everyone knows you treat a fever with fresh chicken soup, so the farmer took his hatchet to the farmyard for the soup's main ingredient. But his wife's sickness continued, so friends and neighbors came to sit with her around the clock. To feed them, the farmer butchered the pig. Unfortunately, the farmer's wife did not get well; she died. So many people came for her funeral; the farmer had the cow slaughtered to provide enough meat for all of them. The mouse looked upon it all from his crack in the wall with great sadness. So, the next time you hear someone is facing a problem and think it doesn't concern you, remember — when one of us is threatened, we are all at risk.

— Anonymous

Growing up in the suburbs, I was always told to represent. Represent yourself, your church, your family, and your race. I was taught to be the model of success. As a college-bound varsity letter winner, I believed that by paying the black tax, working twice as hard, I would be successful. My brothers and sister, my parents and I would strive and rise past the underhanded comments, the snide remarks of our peers, to carve out an assumed reality of success. And alter reality we did — evident in the misconceptions and bizarre remarks of our peers. As my high school lab partner told me, "You are not your typical soul sister." Whatever that meant; my honorary acceptance card, I suppose. It may never be fair, but we were taught that double the effort and humility leads to merit…maybe.

I remember going to the mall late on a rainy Saturday afternoon. It was cool and damp. My family had run the typical errands, purchasing socks for gym class, a new pair of canvas Nikes with that cool blue swoosh. The mall was packed with kids from my local high school. The arcade rang loudly with pinball, and the new fangled electronic bass "bloop bloop bloop" of Space Invaders and Asteroids served as the typical backdrop next to the cinema with kids winding around the corner for the matinee. I could not wait to get home. Home: safe with a fire place, homemade chili, and the latest cop show I'd watch with Daddy. As my family and I made our way to the exit, I noticed kids from my school, the wrestling team, puffed up in their woolen varsity jackets, shifting their weight, toggling that can of Skoal tuck and chew tobacco across their worn Levi's jeans rear pockets. They had this hip long-hair with Aerosmith vibes; everyone wanted to know them, even more so than the football team. A circle of blonde girls with Farrah Fawcett hair and glitter looked on them fondly, almost cooing through their pastel pink lip gloss.

Then, like a ricochet of sound, the words fly, suspending the cacophony of mall traffic. "GO HOME NIGGERS." This was the late 70s. We were not a community forced into busing, perhaps because there were not enough blacks to bus anywhere. The words, while brief, punctuated the thick damp air, "GO HOME NIGGERS." Then it was gone, the moment, the shock, leaving behind a footprint of shame on my heart. Who else were they talking to? There were no other people of color for miles. Will I ever fit in? Will they ever see my family as people, not automatons of color or race? I am supposed to turn my head to my father as he took my hand to guide us through the crowd to the exit. My mother's eyes stayed straight, alert, focused on composure. Her hand was on my brother's shoulder, pointing him sternly to the exit, and my younger brother followed the lead. We exited, without dropped heads, without a break in our gait or a ripple of acknowledgement. We exited that moment in time that rang loudly in our ears, and silently in the car ride home.

Just as my family walked out of that mall, never to acknowledge to ourselves or each other that hurtful racist event, we chose to ignore other racial tensions. We tried to believe that we have overcome, that it is our imagination. We had moved to the best neighborhood, drove nice cars; our token existence validated the emerging hope that our communities could grow out of what one black leader calls America' racist birth defect. We wanted to give people the benefit of our doubt. Even that moment, "NIGGERS GO HOME," was a moment, a blip on the screen that froze in time in my mind, anyway. And then we glossed over it, deciding not to make waves, wanting to be accepted. Let's face it; I had school on Monday, my brothers were trying out for the school play, and my older sister had a birthday party. Would we lose our precarious acceptance by making a stink over a verbal slur that had come and gone in moments?

In this environment, we continued our humble and penitent pose. The goal was always to be the very best. Both of my brothers and my sister emerged from suburbia as honor students, college-bound. Among the four of us, we were three-sport letter winners and one of us was a junior deacon in our church. We played seven instruments, participated in ten musicals, lettered in five sports, held six student government offices, eventually spoke four languages and never missed Sunday school. At every achievement, every moment under the sun, my mother had our picture in the local paper — dean's list, regional champs, honor band, and a list of academic and artistic achievements to endorse our worth, or value. We strove for perfection in an imperfect world. My mother often dubbed us the Huxtables of Hastings Valley. We were model integrationists.

The downside is the emotional front, the mask we donned to make the walk through acceptance. When prom time came, my sister and I had our dates "imported." My father drove miles to the next big city to pick up the son of his fraternity brother. There would be no interracial dating at my high school. My brother was smart and had group dates, a bunch of friends went, but none paired with a single person, no boy/girl couples, just a group of people staying well within the "friend zone."

The perfection continued well into our bachelor's and graduate degrees. In fact, my sister turned down medical school to go to graduate school. My younger brother sought his Ph.D. in comparative literature, while my oldest brother developed his own IT consulting firm. There are three Ivy League degrees between us, all earned on fellowship. All of us are proud college graduates from the nation's top schools — each and every credential immortalized in print for the world to see and accept. These endless articles noted our arrival to mainstream society once and again, and every time.

Excellence was commonplace; the image of what any family would want, regardless of race. Our bubble was seemingly unruptured until we were well into our careers. Somewhere between being the bright neophyte on the job, which yielded the confident and consummate professional, we had masked racial identity with Ivy pigskin and fine German cars.

Young, gifted, and black people were acceptable and even honored at the entry level. The malleable minority is the perfect affirmative action pet for the liberal institution trying to reaffirm its public commitment to diversity. Our respective careers flourished in the first six to eight years. Yet the attainment of degrees and experience made the climb to professional notoriety all the more steep. What once seemed like a steady climb up the easy grade, suddenly changed to feeling the need for hooked boots and climbing gear to scale the cliff's edge of employment.

My eldest brother's response was to leave the traditional ascension of success. He sought to create his own firm, be his own boss. His stories echoed in my mind of how his boss would privately praise his work in IT development, yet publically give credit to the division. My eldest brother played this game for seven years, watching colleague, after trainee, after intern get promoted up and out of his area on the information he gave them through training. But in his hushed tones, he gathered his resources, and gathered his client list, and made a break for his own start-up IT group. We thought at first he was crazy. But his early onset diabetes symptoms subsided; he seemed happier, and simply went from the Benz to a Volkswagen. As his own boss, he groomed that company into a sizeable force in a mid-sized Southeast market. He no longer has to remake himself or his professional persona to meet the needs of an insecure boss who was handpicked as the company's fair-haired favorite to run the division.

My eldest sister, quiet and proud, had the highest test scores in the state. Mother said it was all that brain food she ate during her pregnancy. My sister was a goddess in my eyes. She stood like a surreal picture for me. I would watch her on a late sticky spring afternoon, as she rounded the track in her relay. She didn't flinch to take the field and hurl that javelin into first place to score those extra points. She was my she-ro, my Wilma Rudolph, my Flo Jo, and a Loraine Hansberry as well — young, gifted, and black. Despite my mother's prodding, she chose not to stand down front, but let her accomplishments speak for themselves. If I was the apple of my father's eye, she was the queen; and I would follow her anywhere to be in her court.

My sister graduated from Princeton in three and a half years, took an internship in Washington DC, and worked with a professor to coauthor a white paper on public policy. Her career seemed to be taking off a few years later, with a full graduate scholarship to Northwestern. I missed her while

I finished my own Bachelor's degree. We talked often, but what was once a daily treasure slipped into a weekly obligatory call. She became distant, quiet, focused, almost hurt. I chalked it up to the pressure of her master's studies, being far away, in a new city. When we saw her at Thanksgiving, we were all shocked. My sister had shifted her appearance, wearing masculine clothes, dark blues, grays, nothing like the jewel tones that we knew her by, and donned a particularly expensive weave. My younger brother teased her, staying she was the Brooks Brothers' black Barbie. She just returned a cold stare, "Chicago is cold even in the fall." My father's body language remarked on her distance as he passed the black eyed peas.

Later that evening, after mother turned in, my sister was talking with my father in his study. She had a jerking cadence to her talk, her posture slumped, defeated. "C'mon in Sweetie," my father said to me as I deliberately walked at a snail's pace past the open door. "You need to learn these lessons too." My sister gave me a hug, and we sat together on the couch across from Daddy. She told of her clinical position in downtown Chicago. She needed it for field credit to finish her degree. I didn't know how much she hated it until she opened her mouth to tell of her workplace. Her boss, an elderly white lady from old Chicago politics, would nag her. The woman would purposely insist on meeting at lunch, and talk about her behind her back to other employees. She mocked my sister's Princeton degree, commenting Princeton just let women in recently, that SHE could not go as a girl from Chicago. The haranguing was slow at first, but as winter grew near, the office grew colder. My sister was strong yet hurt, repeating her tale of finding fried chicken on her desk, though she is a well-publicized vegetarian. Despite her first spectacular year in the office, her co-workers now stayed away from the line of fire she was drawing. But my sister wasn't a quitter. While we all knew this was racism, and we knew it was not so overt to make a big stink. My father commented that she should "keep her nose to the grindstone, finish the assignment." She was evolving into a threat, educated and beautiful.

I was startled, and understood why I had not heard from her. I could see it was hard enough for her to tell the story once, let alone repeat it week after week to her little sister. She had a quandary; her spirit was large and bold enough to fight through the hurt. Our mother had always told us to speak up and out. And while she would follow my father's advice to finish the assignment, she also documented every sly remark, chicken bone, and banana that showed up on her desk. She recorded the stories of other workers of color who faced the same tyranny from this lady over the next two months. My sister also found a professor to register her for a research project for extra credit, accelerating her graduation date.

Though she was slated to stay through the following July to finish her internship, she graduated early, and left Chicago to return home. She had filed an EEOC complaint for the harsh treatment she and several others faced at the hand of the elderly Chicago matron boss. My sister's enthusiasm, while not shattered, was shaken. She, like me, had believed that merit, not the color of her skin, would win her favor. She believed still that achievement was the key to equality. She returned substantially heavier — perhaps eating all those Chicago pizzas for comfort — her weave gone, her pinstripes faded, but still with the glint of determination that I saw once when she rounded the track in her relay. My sister was down, but not out, fighting and never to be forgotten.

* * * * * *

Perhaps my youngest brother should have been in that room with us, noting how even these high powered degrees provide minimal deflection from the hate in discrimination. My brother was an idyllic kid. The white girls asked him out frequently; he was the captain of our baseball team, and was vice-president of the honors society. The seas of trouble seemed to part for my brother as he was sweet, talented and an all around good guy. Even the girls in my class would ask who he was dating, or where he was going. As the youngest child, he had a charmed life. The older three had already worn down our parents, and the teachers. He was the last of a great line of kind hearted, creative high achievers. The world was his oyster.

In addition to his athletic gifts, he was a whip in the sciences. He went to the governor's program for two summers for math and chemistry, and developed various models for the state-wide science fair. He was my mother's favorite, meaning she quietly cried her eyes out when he accepted his scholarship to Massachusetts Institute of Technology for college. He was drawn to a renowned professor who had left Bell labs and brought a laser to campus. My brother was one of three students recruited from across the country to help this professor rebuild the laser to operational status. He was living on campus, next to the lab; everything was right at his finger tips.

During his junior year, he decided to save scholarship dollars and move off campus. He left the protective bubble of Cambridge and moved across the Charles River to Roxbury. He called himself savvy and mature, saving money and being a member of the community. My father reluctantly said nothing, figuring my brother had to grow up some time. The term started out routinely: crisp fall mornings, a quick jaunt to the orange line then the red line, and on to Cambridge. He was working later hours developing his thesis idea. Just after Thanksgiving, my younger brother called me; his apartment had been ransacked and searched by the Boston Police Department. He was ashamed, hurt, and downtown in a holding cell. My mind was racing, why did he choose me? He didn't want to alert Daddy, who would come in there like gang busters. He had showed his MIT ID, but the police booked him anyway.

Apparently some high society executive from Newton claimed that he and his wife had a fight leaving the Copley Center. Allegedly she had jumped from the car in tears, and wandered the streets of Boston at night. Of course, the police just knew some 'brotha' had taken her in, and kept her against her will. Several apartments in my brother's neighborhood were searched that night. He was caught coming home late and "matched the description." I was in my first job and had some money to send him. We agreed to work out the details in the morning.

My brother finished that semester in the neighborhood, but quickly made arrangements to move back to campus for the following spring. When our family gathered at Christmas, I noticed his demeanor had changed, solemn as if a part of him had died, as if he had returned from war, refusing to tell the story of how he won his purple heart. No smiles from him, not a joke or overwrapped present. He sat close to my mom, who was lapping up the extra attention. He told me later while we were shoveling snow that it was the worst night of his life. There were no charges, but some words exchanged, blows exchanged, confidence challenged and lost. He had elected not to tell our folks, but just return to campus. Mom and Dad thought Roxbury was too dangerous and too far anyway. He commented, "I moved to the hood, sure, but who knew the criminal element was really the cops?" The corners of his mouth turned up a bit at his own dry humor. The cold winter wind could not even sweep the words away.

* * * * * *

I reflected on the coming-of-age incidents of my siblings. We had remade, rehashed, reclassed ourselves into anything successful to present well publicly, while crying softly and silently. Our parents had taught us that success breeds success. They had done well early, seeking out master's and doctoral degrees at the local state university. They were among the first in their families and neighborhood to escape big steel and the black lung poisoning of coal mining to refashion a new path of achievement.

Perhaps I was delusional, in some naiveté, thinking I might be exempt from the very personal pain of institutionalized racism. Could I even be exempt growing up in Hastings Valley, watching race riots on the six o'clock news with my tin of caramel popcorn, smacking my lips, intently watching the screen?

I thought Harvard and Stanford and Dartmouth would mask my blackness, my marginalized mainstreamed life, my "otherness." I believed even for a minute that the doctoral hooding ceremony, the three-striped velvet robe might have erased my status, even if just on paper. Hey we have a brotha` in the White House; Jim Crow has gone to bed. Right? Actually, Jim Crow lies right under the covers, still chocking off the dreams of the different and disenfranchised.

Was I exempt, not sitting in, standing down, marching around Washington? Is this my march? My protest? My voice of everyone lifting to sing, no! Not today! Did I believe these moments had passed in history? Did I see them morph into another battle? The stories of my siblings ring loudly in my heart, suspending us in disbelief that my parents were wrong on this occasion, or maybe they just led us to a reality that has yet to be. I drift off to sleep knowing my pillow is not filled with silky white down, fluffed up for a peaceful night's sleep. It is filled with the coarse crow's feathers, scratching my consciousness, my subconscious — and my siblings' stories are mild, a simple lock up, workplace harassment, no one lost life or limb, no one was evicted into the stark streets of poverty and homelessness. We were wounded, and mildly at that, but not wanting for the basic needs of shelter and food.

In all these stories, and the stories of others, administratively lynched, hung out to dry financially, in the root of such pain is shame; shame to be victim still and again, a victim despite the "progress" we made. How can this happen to me? When the brown soul emerges to take its place on the stage of pomp and circumstance, when that soul moves to be equal and embrace society without fear, it emerges often hoping to shed the confines of difference. We have moved passed that. Is MLK's dream realized? We even have a national holiday, right? And when your family depends on you for the mortgage, a car note, or groceries, how do you come home and tell them you have been caught behind enemy lines. How do you explain you were fired and exposed as the presumed unruly nigga` with your Cole Haan bag, packing that ultimate driving machine with your personal belongings in 20 minutes under the supervision of public safety escorting you off the grounds? No amount of tears will clean away the sting of difference, that indelible malady or colorable inconvenience. And the next day, sitting atop your degrees and accomplishments, you are still 'other,' hurt, and left rebuilding your psyche out of the rumble left in the wake of discrimination.

I reflected more on these stories, the ones on the news, in the papers, on the internet. The stories of black and brown people, stories of women, those in language and religious minorities, still fighting for the perception of equal treatment, and then I turn under the covers and think.

I reflect even more on the elderly, and the disabled. We all sit in the margins; all have been told to stay in our places. I was once told to wait, wait your turn, stay in your place. I find us all still waiting for this so called post racially reality that supposedly dawned with the first black president.

* * * * * *

My hurt, our hurt, is not isolated or unique, only redundant. In this year, 2011, that I stop and reflect, I read that job discrimination claims will exceed those claims of last year. The regional EEOC offices are on pace to exceed the number of complaints filed. In 2009, retaliation complaints were at an all time high. During such a tough economy, layoffs and furloughs, some people in the dominant culture return to their original state of mind, unfortunately; acceptance and tolerance of difference races, if ever achieved by American society, is only an idea. Race discrimination, gender discrimination, discrimination for those with disabilities, all have a higher rate of complaints. The complaints filed in 2009 exceeded those in 2008, and the last three years eclipse any volume of filings since the EEOC was founded in 1965, with race discrimination being the leading reason for complaints For the fiscal year 2010, private sector workplace discrimination charge filings with the EEOC hit an unprecedented level of 99,922. Retaliation surpassed race as the most commonly filed complaint while the EEOC secured over $404 million for victims. These pervasive stories of discrimination are spawned from fear, leaving pock-marked shame and hurt on a beaten heart of the victims who were only striving to be better; discrimination stifles creativity, progress, and the general propensity to love and be loved.

In my reflection, I think of other men and women who have endured such disrespect after refashioning and reinventing themselves to fit into an institution or organization that never saw them for the beauty they were in the first place. The people I know all continue the drive for excellence, and self-sacrifice, for a company that shook them off. Commonly, they all hurt, yet moved on in spite of it. Discrimination is over.....right?

Chapter 2

Sondra Wilson—Jim Crow flies to Motown

The EEOC reported a 35% jump in the number of complaints filed from the data reflecting 2007 to 2008. Racial discrimination is the most frequently alleged charge of harassment and discrimination under federal law. Several states and some large cities also have anti discrimination laws. Section 1981 of the Civil Rights Act of 1866 and Title VII of the Civil Rights Act of 1964 are the primary federal laws governing racial discrimination.

Sondra Wilson was a grand-daughter of the Old South, raised with a second cousin, Jim Crow not quite twice removed. She watched her uncle sprayed with fire hoses when he was in a sit-in at the local petro station. She watched with eyes wide, glossy with tears that magnified the hate blacks experienced in that hottest summer in Tennessee. She remembers the dinner they had; her mother had wrung the neck of her prized hen to celebrate casting her first ballot in any election even though the election was merely for city council. After years of cowering by the radio, grandma proudly got to vote for the first time at the age of 76.

Sondra remembers those Tennessee evenings. Hot and anxious. Her mother told her never to stray off the porch. This was doubly true for her two brothers. During those summer nights they would see the sky, dark and clear, scattered with stars, almost like promises. With the ice clinking in the lemonade, Sondra always said, "I'm gonna go far from here, far so I can see the stars from the bridge, from a building, from a moving car. The stars are for everyone. We should see them from everywhere."

Sondra's teenaged memories were kind, given her parents' care and temperament, but always had that undercurrent of fear, ready to reach out and snatch back the Negro, drown the dark people in despair, ignorance, or just plain complacency. Her uncle was a sanitation worker, but always went off to work clean and crisp, with a shirt and tie. He saved to buy a 1954 T-Bird, with the circle headlights and tail fins, such a pretty car. Sondra remembers fondly those scattered road trips through the south to visit relatives in the Carolinas. Despite their classy ride, bagged lunches were the fare. The corn field was an endless restroom, ambling past sharecroppers' shacks, and the scowled faces of poor whites who resented her uncle's T-Bird. With a childhood marked with race problems, Sondra felt insecure on her porch in the segregated south.

Even after years of watching Sondra's wanderlust from that porch, Sondra's mother cried when she married Melvin Wilson and followed her new husband to Detroit, Michigan. Despite the riots in the north — Newark, Boston, Chicago — the Big Three were booming. Motown was emerging as a colored kingdom of grace notes and chrome; slick men sported that "conk" and worked for the outside promise of a life those white kids had dancing on Dick Clark. Anything was better than the threat of hanging like strange fruit in the hottest harvest of the South.

Sondra's life was simple at first. She and her husband had a small apartment, their first child, and then their second. She returned to night school for college, and graduated Magna Cum Laude with a dual degree in English and Psychology. Her life in the North blossomed from that of full time mother and wife to educator. She became vice-president of the Urban League, and a life member of Delta Sigma Theta. She became noteworthy in town and was invited to join the Links. With Melvin's support, she saved up enough money to join this prestigious group of African-American women leaders. American families were moving from the one- to the two-car household. America's love affair with the automobile helped many auto workers move across town from cool water flats to single family homes in the suburbs. The kids were lined up for a better high school, and Sondra started working part-time at the local elementary school as a substitute teacher. She soon earned a full-time permanent substitute position when a teacher went out on a last-minute maternity leave.

Her career started as an elementary teacher; she performed well, and over the years, she advanced to the head of her department. Her students returned year after year, confirming that she had touched their lives, made them think, and consider the world on their own terms. She recruited a few other teachers of color and ascended to vice-principal. Jim Crow had seemingly flown away from Sondra's bubble outside Detroit, Michigan. What had seemed like a blink of an eye was actually 24 years. Both her children had graduated from the school district; one went on to Michigan State, while the other enlisted in the service. Her husband had retired three years before with a respectable pension. Sondra was slated for retirement in a year, and looking forward to starting the next part of her life, traveling with Melvin.

If the first 24 years of service was a blink, the last year was a never-ending nightmare. The State Department of Education was reviewing several school districts across the state. Sondra's school had a solid track record of graduation and career placement, but other schools in her district, closer to the city, were not as successful. Some changes came abruptly with the appointment of a new school superintendent tasked to clean up the district. Radical changes were on the horizon.

The change came quickly. Sondra's principal of 15 years, Mr. Halston — Hal — an African-American male in his early 60s, was let go two weeks before school started. He had supported the district through desegregation, busing, and a series of racially-charged public relations nightmares. Hal was not only a fixture, he was an icon in Detroit public education. Despite his exemplary record, he was handed his hat when the new administration took over. He received a thank you, a commendation, and his retirement package intact. At their last lunch together, Mr. Halston reminded Sondra, "You only have to make it a year, actually September through May. Sondra, you're good, so they need someone in the school to provide consistency while they transition over, but call me if you need me."

Sondra asked, "Hal, how are you taking all this?"

"I wasn't planning on retiring this year, but the kids are glad. Since their mom died I have thrown myself into my work. I'll visit them, and my grandchild on the way."

Sondra exclaimed, "Well, congratulations, you'll be a great granddad."

"There's a time and season for everything. It is my time to move on, even if I needed a push to get on with it." The sides of his mouth turned up slightly; he was trying to make the best of it.

* * * * * *

The first day of school was full of unexpected events. The new principal, Dr. Andrew Bernard, a chubby white male in his late 40s, marched into the all school assembly with the new superintendent on his heels, Dr. Eli Peppers. Dr. Peppers was also a white male, from some large school system in the south. For a man in his early 60s, he was a bit colorful for the north with pastel seersucker suits and a wide brimmed linen hat out of season for the brisk September in Michigan. This appointment was apparently his last hurrah in education.

As the teachers were filing in with their classes and filling the auditorium, the two new school administrators took the stage, walking right past Sondra. She walked over to them and handed them the agenda. She noted to Dr. Bernard that there was a program and the school band was excited to play on the first day; they had been practicing for two weeks in their free time. Dr. Bernard almost snatched it away and looked at it over his half moon glasses.

"Humph…" He leans to the superintendent, "See what I am working with?"

Sondra recoiled, and realized the agenda had now changed.

Dr. Bernard folded the agenda and tucked it neatly in his jacket. As the students finished taking their seats, his face shifted to a smile. He patted the head of the microphone and cleared his throat. "Good morning Saginaw Middle School!" The students cheered as they did every year, as if on cue."

"Good morning! I am so excited to be here. I am Dr. Bernard, your new principal. We are entering a new era here at Saginaw and I am so thrilled you will be a part of it. We are focusing on academic excellence — our theme is

PREPARING YOU FOR THE NEXT LEVEL. We will have extra tutoring, more parent conferences and other programs to help you succeed. My door is always open!"

Sondra thought to herself, Dr. Bernard hasn't seen the budget yet. He is making promises without meeting with the teachers' union, or administrative staff.

Dr. Bernard then cued the band director unexpectedly. "So, my esteemed teachers, back to your classes, I will visit with all of your classes, and you as well." At Dr. Bernard's cue the band started up, the strained middle school flutes and wailing clarinets signaling the end of the program. The band eked out an adolescent version of *When the Saints Come Marching In*. The teachers were startled but got the cue to exit their students. They were expecting at least a 45-minute program as they had every year. Sondra approached Dr. Bernard and Dr. Peppers.

"Did you see the program? Each class had a small opening day presentation."

Dr. Bernard had realigned his glasses. "We'll talk, Mrs. Wilson."

"What should I tell the teachers? They…."

Dr. Bernard cut her off, removing his glasses abruptly, "We'll get to this later in my office."

Sondra felt humiliated in front of the new superintendent, who simply stood back and said nothing. She saw the befuddled looks on teachers' faces as they filed out. The culture had definitely changed, and she was not considered as a part of the new team.

* * * * * *

That fall was the season of Bernard's malcontent. He simply ignored Sondra for two months. He took over faculty meetings, and he alone set the agenda for the fall teachers' in-service training. He was running the school without absolutely no input or support from Sondra Wilson. She found that more overt things started happening. She came to work on Saturday morning to clear up a few reports for the state, only to find the locks changed. When she asked on Monday morning what happened, Dr. Bernard simply commented, "You have no business here on Saturday; what you do is not that important. You need to give me the reports to submit to the state so I know what is going on."

Sondra found that her computer was taken one day, without notice. Her inquiry again was met with hostility, "Obviously you are not up-to-date on technology. Your machine was four years old. EVERYONE needed an upgrade." Dr. Bernard scoffed, "That is something I needed my vice-principal to handle, but since you didn't see it, maybe you are too old for the job. I took it on myself. Oh, and you better not waste district time talking to your son in Guam either." Sondra was startled. Dr. Bernard never called an operations meeting, never told her of plans to upgrade machines, or about the changed locks. The last meeting she had on the topic was with Hal, when the message was that the school district was placing a hold on upgrades because of budgets. And her son in Guam? No one knew that. Her son had just been reassigned two weeks previous and he called through on the district line once to wish Sondra a happy birthday, for all of five minutes. She realized that she was not only being scrutinized, but watched — tracked, in fact.

The pressure mounted coming into Thanksgiving. Dr. Bernard had cancelled the diversity programs around Thanksgiving. The school had worked for years to make the programs more inclusive, instead of the traditional Native Americans sitting around in feathers while the Pilgrims made gourmet meals. He cancelled the holiday schedules, too; the school presented programs regarding the Chinese New Year, Ramadan, and different religious celebrations around the world. Sondra hated to ask him about it, but the teachers were complaining that he was a tyrant who changed their work and programs without warning. Some of the black teachers were already coming to Sondra asking for references. Two were willing to take lower-paying jobs in the next district over just to get out of Dr. Bernard's building.

Once again Sondra got up the nerve to speak to Dr. Bernard in his office. "The teachers are really upset with the changes in their programs. We…I mean, they spent a lot of time on those…"

Dr. Bernard cut her off… "Look, this is exactly the type of mentality I am working so hard to change. It is about progress, test scores, promotion, not cupcakes and parties. I have been watching your leadership, Sondra, and it leaves a lot to be desired. Maybe take this upcoming Thanksgiving weekend to think about how you can turn it around."

Sondra again was shocked. She knew better than to rebut. Instead, she simply nodded and returned to her office. Her next call was to her attorney. He knew of some of the problems. Sondra was six months away from the finish line of retirement, and now wondered if she could make it.

* * * * * *

Melvin and Sondra met with their long-time family friend and attorney, Bart Rafferty. He was a stocky, run of the mill white guy. He used to play farm league hockey like most Michigan boys growing up, until an injury kept him from going pro. So he went to law school and was a fierce competitor. Melvin, Sondra, and Bart had worked through the Detroit Urban League together. He had come to their kids' christening. They stood by him when his brother was killed in a car accident. Bart even came to speak at Sondra's sorority about financial planning and retirement. He was a good guy, with a good heart, and with integrity of gold.

"Sorry to catch up with you under these circumstances," Bart said as he opened the door of his office.

Melvin replied, "Glad you could meet us on short notice. Sorry to take up your Thanksgiving weekend. I am really concerned for Sondra."

Sondra continued, "It is just a nightmare. I am trying to get to retirement, which is only four months away." Sondra retold her stories of Hal's forced retirement, the opening day assembly, and the changes in programming and responsibility. The fact that she was never consulted. Her opinions were never considered. Dr. Bernard didn't change locks and take computers from the white staff. He didn't condescend to anyone else except Sondra. In fact, he seemed to take great pleasure in serving Sondra such put downs in public. In contrast, the chair of math department, a white male, got more respect and consideration than Sondra. The math chair received a new secretary, but when Sondra's administrative assistant left abruptly, there was no budget for a replacement. The math chair was asked to serve in the principal's place at meetings, and received invitations to represent the school to the press on occasion. All of these duties had been handled by Sondra.

Bart said, "You are going through what I would consider a constructive discharge. He has not fired you yet, but in his mind he has. He has shut you off, stripped you of duties and responsibility, and speaks condescendingly to you in front of staff and students. Have you complained to HR yet?"

Sondra was dreading this option. She only had four months; she just wanted to leave peacefully. "I see what you are saying… "

"And I have to ask this Sondra: why do you think this is happening?"

Melvin blurted out, "Bart, man, can't you see?"

Bart turned to Sondra, saying, "Mel, let her answer."

Sondra lifted her eyes and looked directly at Bart with determination, "I believe I am being harassed because of my race and age. No other white person is receiving the same disgraceful treatment that I am receiving on a daily basis. No man is facing this either."

Bart continued, "You need to be clear on that point. You need to SAY it. This is about racial harassment and age discrimination. Write up something and fax it to me tonight. It is imperative that when you return to work on Monday you go on record that you are feeling harassed because of your race and sex."

Melvin held Sondra's hand. "You know you have my full support."

Bart stood up and crossed the room to light a cigar to ease his own tension about the situation. "Good Melvin, she's gonna need it."

Sondra continued, "All these years, sit-ins, lock outs, strikes. I grew up in the segregated South. I thought I had gotten away. Now four months before retirement I gotta fight."

Bart was now more relaxed, with a haze of cigar smoke floating around his head, "This fight came to you because you could fight it."

Sondra and Melvin stood; Sondra extended her hand to Bart, "Thanks again for this time on your holiday."

Bart reminded her, "If one of us has a problem we all do. I look forward to your fax."

* * * * * *

First thing Monday, Sondra Wilson reported to the central district office instead of her own building. She was hand carrying her complaint to HR.

As a 24-year veteran of the district, everyone knew her. "Good to see you Sondra! Did you see the Lions on Thursday? They lost AGAIN! What a Thanksgiving. Coming in to talk retirement?"

Sondra only nodded and walked through the office. She entered the director's office and quietly handed her the note. Kathleen Winters and Sondra had been colleagues for years. Sondra tried to ease the blow. "I was trying to just retire. There is nothing to meet about, and a copy of this letter is coming via certified mail, too."

Kathleen opened the note and read it. She dropped her eyes and re-read the letter. When she finished she simply said, "Sondra, I understand. We will look into it."

All the gracious talk, chatter about football and leftovers, were left at the door. This was serious.

Sondra quietly stood, her eyes determined yet quiet, and extended her hand. "Well, I gotta get back to my building."

Kathleen nodded and then handed Sondra her business card, with her home number on the back. "I think you have this, but just in case."

By the time Sondra crossed the district to report to work, it seemed her entire building knew. Some of the teachers smiled from a distance as Sondra entered the building. The secretary's hushed tones came to a dead silence as Sondra walked in. Dr. Bernard was in his office with the door closed. Sondra had peace; it was awkward in the principal's suite, but he left her alone for almost two weeks.

Sondra had not heard a word from Kathleen Winters in HR. She was happy to have what she realized to be the calm before the storm. The teachers were getting ready for their Christmas pageant, the one thing Dr. Bernard did not cancel. Sondra had hoped that her complaint would give her enough time to make it to May. She was wrong. Just after the pageant, Dr. Bernard called a private meeting with her.

"I have been very disappointed in you, Sondra. I have watched you sequester yourself in your office. You seem to be available only to certain teachers. You seem to be more concerned about parties than achievement test scores. I am letting you go. You are being separated from the district this afternoon."

Sondra heard a ringing in her head, "I... I am only four months from retirement, Dr. Bernard."

"That is not my problem. My problem is test scores and adequate yearly progress. What you are doing is not at all part of my administration. We can't wait four months just to keep you on until you retire. What about the kids, what about the parents who depend on us. It's not about your retirement; it is about my administration." Dr. Bernard paused to look Sondra dead in the eye.

"I will pay you for this last week before Christmas. But starting January 1, you are no longer employed here. I have made arrangements for you to get your personal items over the weekend. Security will let you in." There was a pause; Sondra's disbelief was suspended in the air. "Sondra, I need your keys before you leave."

Sondra started to protest, then simply gathered her notepad and returned to her office. She took the two pictures of her kids, and her coat. She was glad the secretarial pool was gone for the day. Her hands shook as she dressed for the cold. FIRED after 24 and a half years of service.

In the car on the way home she called Mel. "Can you believe this?"

Mel replied, "Let's talk when you get home. You know to call Bart. Call him."

Sondra's next call was to Bart, who almost seemed to be waiting. He listened to her and then responded, "So are you ready to move forward for real?"

"Yes..."

"I'll be over for dinner. Tell Mel to break out the Glenlivet too."

Over dinner, Bart, Mel and Sondra had a quick reminiscence about the Detroit Urban League, their fight to desegregate the YWCA downtown, the town meetings regarding police brutality and the city supervisor who said Detroit was full of "N-gg-s."

Sondra was humbled by their past accomplishments, "So we fight on."

Mel and Bart tipped their glasses, ice clinking in the amber scotch.

Bart reviewed the EEOC complaint forms with Mel and Sondra. It was simple yet concise. The strategy: to fight for the right thing. Get this to the EEOC first thing Monday morning, and messenger a copy to Dr. Bernard, the superintendent, Dr. Peppers, and include a statement that Sondra is prepared to go to the press. They took a couple hours to compile information, timelines and a few witnesses. They made five copies of the file and agreed to rest well over the weekend.

Bart had been invaluable helping Sondra to fine tune her complaint. "I had hoped it didn't need to come to this. But if we don't use the federal rules, these guys will continue to hurt others. On to round two."

That Monday, Sondra personally sat in the EEOC office to file an official complaint. She had all the forms typed and collated. The intake person stated, "You must be a teacher or lawyer or something. Many people don't come in here so well organized."

Melvin drove by the district office to hand deliver a copy of the complaint to the superintendent's office. He dropped off a copy at Sondra's old building too. The next day, Sondra received written confirmation of her termination in the mail. She was advised about COBRA, and on the waiting period required to file for unemployment. Sondra and Melvin sat down to review their finances and options with this change in the family cash flow.

Two days later, Sondra received a call from Dr. Peppers, the school superintendent. He had read the formal complaint. He stated, "Mrs. Wilson, I am calling for clarification. I believe Dr. Bernard wasn't clear. Your position had been eliminated, meaning you would not be vice-principal, but we still need an assistant vice-principal. You would work three days a week, develop curricula for in-service training, many of the same duties as before."

Sondra just listened.

"Mrs. Wilson, are there any questions? I know you are on paid holiday vacation this week. I just wanted to be clear about your new duties starting January 2nd."

Sondra replied, "I appreciate your goal to be clear. For the sake of clarity, can you put this in writing?"

Dr. Peppers replied, "Certainly, you can expect this in the mail within two days." There was an awkward silence. "I hope you and your family have a good holiday."

The call ended as abruptly as it started. Sondra called Bart immediately.

"Bart, should I take it? I mean is it a demotion? Did we win?"

Bart replied, "You have their attention. They are trying to cover their tracks and call it a business necessity."

"I don't think I want to be in that hostile enviroment. It was really bad the last few months."

"Sondra, go on back in there and get your pay and benefits. You have health and educational benefits. Go back to school on their dime. Take in some conferences. You will be in a better position to fight them from the inside, just like Moses."

Melvin agreed with Bart's legal advice when he got home. Stay in there and fight. So on January 2nd, Sondra returned to her building. The secretary approached her and smiled with discomfort."Hope you had a nice holiday, Mrs. Wilson." The secretary cut her eyes and returned Sondra's keys and ID picture. "Nice to see you back from vacation."

That winter in Detroit was particularly cruel. Dr. Bernard didn't come out of his office often. The teachers were on automatic pilot. No one dared speak to Sondra; she was the school leper. But Sondra took the opportunity to take some online courses for her doctorate. She had even bought her own laptop and air card so she would not use the district server for any business. She did take a week long seminar in Albuquerque, New Mexico. Mel came with her. It was a nice change of pace and she earned another certification.

She was saddened as she received the occasional call at home. Several of the teachers were unhappy; several African-American and Hispanic teachers were leaving. When Dr. Bernard started, there were 17 teachers of color. By Easter, they were down to six. The losses were especially hard in the math and sciences.

The month of May was a relief. The district pretty much closed down, except to prepare for commencement. A central school in the district handled summer school, but Sondra's building was typically quiet.

She called Bart, "I guess I made it. Retirement..."All she wanted was back pay and health benefits.

"No! You must stay until this is over. There are at least another six months for them to investigate. You have summer off as a part-time employee. Make headway with that degree and be prepared to return in the fall. If you retire now, you are retiring as a part time employee, who is not entitled to benefits."

Sondra discussed it with Melvin and quietly consented. She worked feverishly during the summer, earning at least 15 graduate credits. She had a mentor figure in the department in whom she confided. "So many people let this kind of discrimination go; Sondra, I am glad that you are fighting the school district."

The summer provided the respite Sondra needed. A few of her departing teachers met up with her over lunch. They talked about what a horrible principal Dr. Bernard was, and how he thought he was changing the culture for the good. Sure Saginaw had problems, but morale was never one of them. With so many teachers leaving, and others doing the bare minimum to survive the environment, the kids were hurting. Test scores were down 9%, and for the first time they had several openings. The word was out; no one wanted to work at Saginaw Middle School. In the mean time, she had to field a flurry of requests from the EEOC. They needed her personal records that she saved. She still had letters of commendation from Hal. Sondra also had records on how three of her interventions helped students. She had mentored over 25 faculty over the last ten years as they sought their masters.

Fall provided more of the same. Sondra settled into a conference schedule, worked toward her degree, and supported the teachers through in-service. The EEOC had to interview staff and asked for more information, memos, and emails. She and Melvin found money tight, but were still committed to the complaint. In mid-December, one year later, she received her "Right to Sue Letter" from the EEOC. The matter had not been resolved, as many complaints are not resolved within a year.

And Bart was ready: "Well, here we are at the year benchmark. I have a group of attorneys who have been watching your case. You know employment law is not my forte, but I know this group. They will fight hard for you."

On Bart's advice, Sondra went to the Equity Brothers Law Firm. They conducted the standard intake, reviewing her complaint and the EEOC records. They also had a particular interest in the Right to Sue letter. With attorneys officially in the picture, a formal court case was shortly behind them. Within

30 days of filing the case, Sondra's school received the complaint from federal district court, which was served to the school district shortly after the new year.

Sondra was interested in bringing this to closure. Melvin had watched her lose weight and patience. Her hair was thinning and her blood pressure up. Melvin assured her that this was the right thing to do. Her sons also supported her, reminding her, "Don't ever back down mom! Remember you told us that — back down leads to mowed under."

In the long run, Sondra decided not to retire until the case was closed. She waited for the investigation, discovery and various conciliation meetings. The district argued using the statute of limitation doctrine that the incidents had happened over a year ago, while the judge ruled that Sondra was still on-site and still enduring the discrimination. Her attorney was right, staying on at the district made her case.

During that time, her case had hit the press:

VICE-PRINCIPAL SUES SCHOOL DISTRICT
FOR RACE & AGE DISCRIMINATION

Once her case went public, Sondra was initially embarrassed. She never wanted any trouble, just to retire in six months. Why was Dr. Bernard such an idiot? Just six months?

Sondra's sorors rallied around her. They now knew why Sondra had been absent from the meetings for the past year. Some called quietly, while others stopped by unannounced. They enforced the philosophy that strong black women fight. They stand and fight so the girls rising in careers behind them hopefully don't have to fight this fight. Her Delta Sigma Theta chapter asked her to be the keynote speaker at their Red and White Ball. The theme was "Equality and Justice for All." The chapter president reminded her, "we are the education sorority, and we have to educate each other, even on the unpleasant topics."

Sondra received quiet calls from educators in other school districts and a couple universities. They wanted to know about her attorney: Was he good?

Fair? How was she doing? Sondra had become an EEO guru of sorts, giving verbal wisdom to her community on how to fight, and with what tools. Her Links Sisters and fellow Urban League members also showed support in their own ways. An op-ed piece appeared in the *Detroit Times* regarding Sondra's case, encouraging others to come forward when they have similar problems.

Nineteen months after Sondra filed with the EEOC, which was seven months after she filed the case in court, the school district finally settled, offering her back pay from the time she was full-time to part-time. The total was roughly $65,000' a third of this went to her attorney. She received full retirement benefits, and the right to stay on as long as she wished.

A week after she received the certified settlement and 1099 payment, she resigned.

Though she had 26.5 years of service, there were no retirement parties, no roasts, no former students coming back to shower her with praise and accolades. Despite 26 plus years of service, Sondra felt only vindicated to get away with her benefits intact. With this experience, she recommitted herself to sorority and Urban League activities. Others needed to know about the EEOC employment laws and how to protect themselves. She thought retirement was going to be a quiet time of cruises, shopping, and visiting her kids. But even in retirement, she saw the fight was not over. Melvin taught her that. Bart taught her that. She knew without a doubt that Jim Crow flies north as well.

Chapter 3

Raquel Battle—Retaliation from the heart of Texas

If an employer is subject to a retaliation charge, the case may already be lost. Retaliation is a punitive and adverse employment action taken on the part of the employer, after an employee exercises his or her civil rights to complain about harassment on the basis of membership to a protected class, as defined by EEOC Guidelines (race, color, national origin, religion, and sex, pregnancy, disability). An adverse action is not simply termination; changing an employee's shift, a demotion, or change in administrative support can all fall under adverse employment action and under scrutiny if the employee endures these changes after presenting a verbal or written complaint.

Sugarland, Texas was not so sweet for those coming up disadvantaged in greater Houston. As a toddler, Raquel stayed with her father, who worked as a custodian at Imperial Sugar. He was a smart man. He had dropped out of Baylor as a junior in history and economics when he learned that Raquel's mom was pregnant. He was honorable and took responsibility for Raquel's care, as her mother's thirst for recreational drugs continued to increase. The sugar plant was hard work, but it was the best option so he could spend time with Raquel. He smelled of burnt sugar coming home, and he reminded anyone who listened that the sugar plant was originally a sugar plantation in the 1800s. And they still worked the employees like slaves. Raquel's father died as a young man of 50, of diabetes of all things. God has a sense of humor; a sugar plant employee dies of diabetes.

His death brought an instant change of scenery. Raquel was shipped off to her mom's, a some-time resident of Kelly Village in the 5th Ward. Though Raquel grew up in the fourth largest city in the nation, her world seemed so small as a child. She bounced back and forth between Bruce Elementary and Crawford Elementary, if she was staying with her aunt or with her grandmother while her mom was trying to get herself together. Meanwhile, Uncle John, Uncle Jack, Uncle Crack, whoever, paraded through Raquel's life as her mom's newest "friend." The 5th Ward was the worst part of Houston, the Bayou City. Pimps and hustlers dotted the streets. Her grandma bought a new steel door every three years to protect them from random drive-by shootings. In fact, that door saved her little cousin one year. MLK Drive was the most dangerous drag; it was ironic how a street named for peace turned out to be the city's killing zone.

Raquel liked staying with her aunt the best, and it soon became her home. Aunt Grace rode two buses every morning, from the 5th Ward to the 2nd Ward, to work for Maxwell Coffee. Raquel liked going to work with her in the summers, seeing the neon coffee cup on the building emerging in the dawn. Her Aunt Grace was the steadiest figure in her life since her dad died. She was a diehard Houston Astros fan, and she told Raquel that she could be anything she wanted. Look at Ann Richards; she was a woman, a teacher turned state treasurer, and then governor of Texas. Her aunt reminded Raquel how Richards pushed for ratification of the Equal Rights Amendment to the U.S. Constitution. She always remembered that National Women's Conference; it was on the news, that this up and coming woman would bring the amendment forward among the good old boys in Texas. You have to be prepared to fight, as a woman, and as a black woman. Aunt Grace said, "Don't ever lay down like my sister did; don't ever work on your knees for no one. You have more going for you. Don't ever give up and lie down. Don't ever give up."

So it was no coincidence that her aunt came home from work one day with a window of opportunity for Raquel.

"I can get you outta here. You too smart for this life. I don't want you working sugar and coffee — you should be leading, not following."

Raquel didn't quite understand, but she did understand the hope and pain in Aunt Grace's eyes.

"I have a new boss at work. The classiest black lady you ever wanna see. She brought me this program. ABC, A Better Chance, Inc. which helps kids with another way."

"What are you saying, Auntie?"

Her Aunt Grace was excited and sad, "I think you can take this test. Get your records together and take the test and get to a better school. A better life."

That summer, Raquel studied math and English. Her aunt had boxed up some of the college books her daddy left her, which came in handy. Aunt Grace even found a local college student who was home for the summer; she paid the tutor with single dollar bills and apple cobbler. Even the tutor knew that the summer was about changing the life of a young girl.

At 13, Raquel was spared the inner city high school system. She passed the entrance exams, and with the help of ABC, Inc. was lifted from the 5th Ward to St. John's Prep School. Raquel was a lanky girl, athletic, and already 5'9". St. John's Prep School is an independent private day school that caters to exceptional students. At SJS, she was in school with the son of the Japanese Ambassador, two kids whose parents were Senators, and a handful of kids whose parents were in the Congress. Fitting in was hard at first, but she had a knack for field hockey — good as a forward and goalkeeper during her high school years. Raquel was left back a year, but performed well and moved on to graduate in the top 10% of her class. Her Aunt Grace cried to see her walk across that stage to receive her high school diploma. Even her mom came to commencement. She hugged her tightly when the ceremony was over.

"Baby, I don't ever have to worry about you turning out like me. I owe it all to my sister Grace. By God's Grace..."

Raquel hugged her mom and forgave her for all the disappointment, and hugged her aunt who had made a way for Raquel. They took a picture together that Raquel has kept on every desk, from school to work. It was the last time she saw her mom alive. Her mom overdosed a month later in a local gas station bathroom.

Raquel kept up several civic activities with the YWCA, and Honor's Club. She was a top academic recruit to Rice University. She had a partial scholarship in field hockey, two other academic scholarships, and a Pell grant to make up her financial aid package. She continued her activities and sports and graduated *cum laude* in communications. After two summer internships with Inroads, she focused on business and public relations, meeting people in her field and keeping business cards over the years. Raquel stayed in touch with them as she went through college, making occasional visits to keep those networks warm. With her Rice degree completed, she moved on to Tulane for a Ph.D . She finished her doctorate in four and a half years. Her star did not seem to stop rising.

Her career flourished; she was hired by a very bright woman who intended to groom her to become the executive director of a renowned public relations firm back in Houston. Raquel was getting practical experience in analyzing the profit and loss statements, recruiting staff, and forming teams. In her late twenties, Dr. Raquel was traveling all across the southwest. She was benefiting from sound mentorship, and had learned from the best about how to look the part, without looking tacky. Sporting Jones of New York and Lafayette 148, Raquel created a nice image: classy, energetic, smart. She also had a great co-worker in Doug Dravers. He was a bit older, in his mid-50s, with a military haircut. Doug seemed like the edgy redneck type, but he was really down to earth. He was a Desert Storm vet. His war experience helped him remain unflappable on most issues, as nothing is like a forward area. The war gave him a strategic calm that Raquel admired. Raquel was the senior colleague of the two on the organizational chart, but together Doug and Raquel created several initiatives, and at times presented before the board. Raquel's work environment was everything she had worked so hard for. She had great colleagues, a supportive boss, and was paid well. Suddenly, her world went sideways as her mentor was picked off by a head hunting firm, with promises to bring Raquel along to her new job in six months.

On the heels of a wonderful four year period with her public relationship firm, Solar, PR, Raquel was open to learning from a new leader. Doug also was anxious to learn new ideas from the seasoned gentleman coming in. Their hopes of getting an innovative leader were dashed when the company hired Dr. Kent, a four time divorcee who was hired as a favor to a friend in the central office. He was a tall skinny man, athletic, and he thought he was God's gift to younger women. He ran the city marathon every year. He had shocking gray hair, like Steve Martin, but wasn't nearly as kind. His cologne was loud, filling an elevator or any closed quarters, and he sported a trendy Damier Louis Vuitton bag. He was a fashion plate in his Ferragamo shoes, but with no class. Excessive drinking caused him to slur his words, and had no common sense about how to talk to people. The staff in the Houston office was shocked that any public relations firm would choose this as its image. Doug and Raquel both recoiled and started helping themselves and each other to the job boards, extending each other their contacts to help look for a new position.

In the meantime, Dr. Kent picked on Raquel. He said she reminded him of that cute little squirrel from Rocky and Bullwinkle, since she had that big fluffy tail. Raquel couldn't believe the words coming out of his mouth.

"....Rocky, I know you can solve this problem, and I'll be your Bullwinkle! All that fancy education, humph!" Dr. Kent was outrageous in his communication with Raquel.

Under Dr. Kent, eight other African-Americans and Hispanic women fled the company. Doug apparently received a pass — maybe it was his military look, or his stature — but Dr. Kent respected Doug and left him alone. Raquel and Doug both saw the writing on the wall for Raquel. She tried to use her solid reputation across the southwest. She had called her mentor and begged for any possible job opening.

Her mentor empathized and agreed, "You've got to get out of there, but I just haven't been here long enough to bring you on. Can you hang on for three months?"

Raquel was not sleeping, and was grinding her teeth at night. She appeared weathered and unfocused. In an executive meeting, Raquel was reporting expenses for a client mixer held the previous week. She reported on the meals, the guests and outcomes. Dr. Kent started on her again:

"How much did this all cost us, Rocky! I know I didn't approve this. You think you're so smart! You're not the only one with a doctor degree, missy! You might have a body like a cola bottle, but your head's like a box of rocks!"

Raquel commented and stood her ground, "I have my own budget, and I will just put in for it at the end of the month."

Dr. Kent stood up and circled the table behind Raquel, Doug, and three other colleagues. "Don't even bother. You ain't gonna show me up." He looked like some corporate vampire circling the room for executive blood. He pulled out his wallet. "Here, don't even put in for reimbursement." Kent pulled some money out of his wallet and tossed it at Raquel. Doug touched Raquel's shoulder and bowed his head. "Anyone else got anything like this mess Raquel brought us?" No one said anything. The silence choked the rest of the meeting. People looked anywhere, did anything to escape that awkward episode.

Doug approached Raquel quietly at the end of the day.

"Here, you need to do something. We all see he is out to get you. You are the only black woman on the executive staff."

Raquel looked down to see Doug handing her a folder of information.

"I made a few phone calls. I'm a white dude, no one would suspect me. Raquel, this man is running you into the ground. He isn't treating anyone else like this. I swear, if that money he tossed at you had hit the floor, I wouldn't have let anyone stoop to get it. Dr. Kent is out of control. This is the company's anti-discrimination and anti-retaliation policy. Look it over. You can't sit here and take this. You are so much better."

Raquel thanked him, recognizing it was a sign and guidance on what to do next. Ordinarily, Raquel wouldn't think twice about waiting three months for her mentor to hire her away. She had received bonuses and was highly ranked across her field. But the harassment did not slow down. Dr. Kent continued to berate Raquel in front of staff, reschedule meetings so Raquel would miss important directives, and sneak around Raquel's desk looking for damning information.

In the midst of applying to positions at other companies, Raquel also went to her internal contacts, to the Southwest VP. She had originally hoped to have this resolved quietly. But no one would help her because Ken had friends in high places. Raquel had no choice but to go to Human Resources to file an internal complaint. In her complaint, Raquel wrote:

After working with Solar Public Relations Associates for the past four years, I am disheartened to face the constant humiliation and stress that I endure daily, working for and reporting to Dr. Kent. I believe that his public disdain for me is based on race and sex, as no Caucasian is facing this harassment, which is constant and enduring. No man is belittled like I am. I believe my job is in jeopardy, as I believe Dr. Kent lacks the objectivity to work with me as an African-American female employee.

Human Resources was obligated to notify Dr. Kent of the formal written complaint. In response, Dr. Kent played out his own chess move. He scheduled a bogus meeting and made unrealistic demands for statistics, reports and presentations. Others at the last-minute meeting were not called to task like Raquel. It felt like a turkey shoot, unreal, and humiliating. Dr. Kent used the results of the meeting to terminate Raquel with 20 minutes' notice, without true cause. Kent did not even wait for the internal discrimination investigation to run its course.

For the first two weeks, Raquel sat stunned in her condo. She had seen shootings, robberies, and she had even been mugged at gun point. But she had worked hard to get out of a place that treated people like meat, like nothing. She had prepared herself, played by the rules, earned those degrees, and the promotions. Now, because some insecure man came in mocking her, she is in danger of financial disaster.

Raquel's performance in client acquisitions and networking was more than notable. Over the previous 18 months, she had received three bonuses for exemplary work. The company had given her major accolades internally for expanding her region and client base. In fact, not only was she noted at the company, she had spoken at the regional conference for public relations directors and had a great op-ed piece in *US Today*. Her star was once not only rising, but speeding like a comet.

Raquel was too embarrassed to admit that she had been terminated. She didn't call her mentor, or even her aunt. When the mailman came to the door, she didn't even answer as she was embarrassed to be home in the middle of the day.

After a few days of crying, and continuous dates with Jack Daniels and Jim Beam, she realized she had to snap out of it. Her tears were not watering flowers, or even easing the pain. She cleaned up a bit and drove over to Forest Lawn Cemetery. She had not been to her father's gravesite in years. The Texas sun baked her as she wandered through the surface streets. She had brought him some flowers from the local grocery.

Standing in front of the tombstone, she remembered how happy she was just to be daddy's girl. Now her family has been thrown to the four winds; she had never married, and children were not in her plans. She figured what good was marriage and kids? It didn't work for her parents.

She laid the flowers down and just cried for a minute. "Daddy I'm sorry, I never wanted to be a disappointment." She stared at the tombstone through her welled-up eyes. Raquel remembered she was in public — she had to pull herself together.

Strolling away, a thought dashed into her head. Her aunt went on and on about women's rights and Ann Richards. Raquel could not get it out of her head: rights, civil rights.

As she drove home, she remembered the EEOC office, down there on Smith Street. At first she dismissed the idea, but it crept back in her mind. She decided to check out the EEOC website. She took the online assessment, which led her to think that she should continue. She decided to pray on it, and study the process.

A month had passed since her termination. Ironically, Raquel had been living on the bonus money she earned, and waited to seek unemployment. During this period, she also found that Dr. Kent had hired a young white male with only a Bachelor's degree to take on Raquel's duties.

Five weeks after her termination, Raquel visited the Houston office of the EEOC. Her case seemed clear — painful, but clear. She complained, and then she was fired. The next months were nerve wracking. Raquel didn't go out much anymore, afraid to run into family who'd want to know how her high flying career was going. She didn't have the money she used to, no more bonuses or raises. She did find peace in teaching at Houston Community College Northwest the following term. She found that in the class room, she could be herself and get the respect as a teacher that many administrators just didn't get. The time away from public relations also helped her to focus on next steps.

Doug continued to be a huge support to her. He had left Solar, PR shortly after she was fired. He had stood up for Raquel several times while she was on site, and again when the EEOC came to inquire. While he knew the federal statutes were designed to protect him from workplace retaliation, he knew from experience nothing could stop a bullet; he decided to get out the way.

Thirty days after she filed in the Houston EEOC office, she received a letter confirming her complaint, with a case number. She called the EEOC to inquire about next steps, and learned that it would be another thirty days before her employer would respond, acknowledging the complaint, and probably denying any wrongdoing.

Raquel spent the next few months looking for work. She also compiled her witness list, calling each person to see who would be willing to participate in the investigation. Some were delighted to help; others brushed her off the phone and refused to answer when Raquel's name appeared on their caller ID. Once she submitted documents and lists, Raquel waited some more.

As with most cases, life had to go on. Raquel, still gun shy from the experience, continued her teaching. The company engaged in a number of stall tactics, nonresponse to meetings, refusing to meet at initial conciliation sessions. Approximately five months after registering her complaint, the commission scheduled an initial conciliation meeting. Her former employer cancelled the meeting with less than 24 hours' notice. Also, she received notice that the firm had retained its own attorney in the case.

Three months after the first meeting was scheduled, Solar, PR made an offer — a simple $10,000 payment. Raquel refused. She had been earning over six figures, with bonuses and a serious expense account. The $10,000 they offered would not even match her severance package. Raquel learned that Dr. Kent had been fired within eleven months of his hire, with a string of discrimination and harassment complaints in his wake. Though the company was wrong, Raquel's career, and that of three other employees, hung in the balance. She was strapped financially, but knew her case was worth more than $10,000. If it went all the way to trial, it was a $500,000 case.

Raquel dug in her heels and refused to settle. She altered her life style. She weaned herself from the martinis and T-bone steaks every Friday night with friends. Raquel was embarrassed to be bumped out of her tax bracket. She changed the terms of her leased car, and settled for a used car. It wasn't sexy, but it was a living. She also found her way into consulting work for public relations companies. As the months passed, she was able to spend more time with her Aunt Grace, who reminded her that the fight was never easy.

The anniversary of her termination approached. She had once hoped her former boss would hire her away. Instead, her mentor figure withdrew after she heard Raquel was terminated; her excuse was, "We are in a recession, a hiring freeze. But I will keep you in mind."

Raquel found herself calling the EEOC once a month to speak with the investigator for updates. A few other people at Acme had also filed complaints with the EEOC, yet there was little movement. Life at Solar, PR went on, the EEOC was swamped. The case lay dormant.

Eighteen months after her initial complaint, Raquel received another settlement offer, this time for $12,000. Raquel had the same answer: No! Her investigator was growing frustrated, too. She had read the file, she knew Solar, PR was wrong, but the company wouldn't budge. The EEOC moved on with its witness list, calling people at home. A few of the people on Raquel's list had forgotten all about it, and some had moved. But a few, three or four, remembered the entire thing. They talked about Dr. Kent, the Rocky and Bullwinkle stories, and how Dr. Kent had been a racist and sexist from the beginning.

The EEOC demanded files, personnel records, meeting notes, and emails. The paper trickled in, but slowly a very clear case was building. Finally, the EEOC investigator called for mediation and suggested that Raquel retain an attorney for the process. The mediation was arranged at no cost, but the attorney would retain a third of the settlement. Raquel was disgusted. Two years and what seemed to be a thousand calls later, she had to go through this ordeal. But it was time to put this to rest.

Raquel searched the Internet to find an employment attorney. She was hesitant; perhaps she really was a bad employee despite her years of decorated service. During an initial interview with the paralegal, Raquel spilled through the highlights of her experience. She was cautious but clear about her experience. Within 15 minutes she was scheduled to have a phone conference with one of the partners. The following week, she had composed herself. If she was going to fight it, she would fight all the way. Her phone conference with the attorney quickly turned into an office visit. Raquel had never even had a car accident or small claims court proceeding, and she certainly didn't know how to prepare for the meeting. "Just be yourself," the attorney commented.

The attorney took her case on contingency. He spoke with the investigator at the Houston EEOC. Solar, PR had already offered a cursory settlement, and did not want to be found responsible in any circumstance. Raquel had really prepared most of the work.

The mediation started with Raquel's attorney making a statement. Raquel spoke of her hardship, and then the Solar, PR representative had a statement. Raquel was seething, and pleased to have an attorney handle this very emotional process. They dickered over the cause for the termination, and her rights to severance and health care. They reviewed her retirement package and what it would have been if she had stayed. Before long, the discussion moved to 1099s, W-2s, checks, and bank accounts. Raquel and her attorney took occasional breaks to caucus, and found themselves above the curve, but still behind the number Raquel really wanted.

Her attorney stated, "You can keep fighting them, and I will support your choice. But I am telling you, these things can go on for years. They are offering a year and a half pay, plus 9%. If we go to court, you might get 25,000 more than that — three years from now."

Raquel lowered her eyes, deep in thought.

Her attorney continued, "You are a smart lady; you can make that in any given quarter. My advice: put this to bed, recoup your losses, and get your life back."

Raquel felt concession rolling in her spirit, and she nodded in agreement.

Solar, PR and their attorneys wrote up a temporary settlement agreement which would be managed by the third party mediator for the next 45 days. Within three weeks, Raquel and her attorney would get the agreement. Sixty days from that, she and her attorney would be paid.

At first Raquel was mad; she had endured a lot of pain, changed her life, and altered her career. But then she realized that there were several people who were fired who had no recourse, no settlement, and no retribution. She had a blessing and vindication.

The day after mediation, a great weight seemed to lift from her shoulders. She was comfortable and preparing for her next academic term. Her consulting business was moving along with her credentials; she could be her own boss. Then it occurred to her; Aunt Grace had always wanted to see the pyramids. This money would fund a celebration. Raquel made her nest egg, her money market, and some CDs, but she also saw her travel agent, to be Queen of the Nile for a week.

Chapter 4

Jodie Barstowe—An ounce of prevention... rationale for severance packages

Often, the smart move for an employer is to offer a severance agreement, which is something the employee values, but may not be entitled to. The package can include salary, health benefits, or even longevity (a separation date officially documented in the future). In exchange for this severance packet, the employee agrees not to sue the former employer.

Many employers have found that even the well-documented termination is not a guarantee to avoid costly defense in court. A hurt and/or wronged employee can often find weakness in any case, and an attorney to defend him or her. The cost to the employer can easily soar to $50,000- $100,000 in legal fees. The severance agreement can protect against such costs as it includes a full release. For the cost of as little as six weeks' pay and health benefits, the employer can, in short, buy a guarantee and peace of mind that they will not have to defend even a bogus charge by the terminated employee.

She came from a middle class white family in south Florida. Her dad was a CPA, and her mom was once runner-up for Miss Florida—a pretty lady, and now an accomplished homemaker. She knew the value of hard work through her high school jobs and even her time as a cheerleader. Jodie Barstowe was an industrious child, working at the Village of Merrick Park in Coral Gables and delivering newspapers in the mornings. She was also a pretty girl like her mother. Her high school swimming kept her in shape. Her mom was always trying to get her to join the pageant circuit. Her wavy blonde hair and curvy figure got her extra tips as a waitress. But instead of focusing on her looks, she had her heart set on going to the University of Miami. Her dad was convinced that the best bang for the buck was attending Miami Dade Community College for two years and then transferring to a state school. But Jodie convinced her dad that she would work hard, pay for part of it, and work summer jobs. She had done well saving for four years, and maintained a 3.8 grade point average in the honors program. Her dad was impressed.

Her dad was even more impressed with the ROTC scholarship that came through for Jodie at the University of Miami to pursue her own degree in accounting. Life was good, not great, but stable. Jodie continued to work odd jobs while balancing her commuting schedule, financial accounting, and school. Her life's pleasure was Bongo's, the salsa club on South Beach, which she went to once a month. She loved Bongo's. She could cut loose and dance away, with or without someone else. Her girlfriends joined her too. She could always count on Pam and Connie to help her work out the frustrations of college. A few drinks, that rhythmic music and on occasion, they met a guy willing to buy a few drinks.

Her other guilty pleasure was following the Miami Hurricanes. She occasionally made extra money tutoring a few guys from the football team and baseball team. She was good with accounting, and a strong tutor. In addition to $8 an hour, she got occasional tickets to the games. Her friend Matthew was a student trainer and got her in. College was a great time despite the hard work. She and Matthew developed a solid relationship and started dating pretty seriously.

With Desert Storm winding up, Jodie's mom was concerned about her commission; Jodie assured her and Matthew that her duties as a financial officer would keep her firmly in Arlington, VA.

Jodie Barstowe was commissioned June 8, 1991 to the Army and took her first assignment in Arlington. Her time with ROTC fashioned her as a strong and confident woman, an expert in her field, and an excellent officer. Duties took her from the Pentagon to Fort Bragg, and then back to the National College of Defense and Strategy where she learned the trades of federal financial aid.

Through the transition, she and Matthew continued to build their relationship, but he wasn't military. His job as an athletic trainer for the arena league provided a good salary, but put him on the road, too. They were determined to stick it out; they married early at 24, and had one son, Calvin. Matthew and Jodie struggled to stay together, but Jodie's travels put a strain on their marriage and three years later, divorce became a part of her challenge. She was hurt, but she relied on her father for moral support, and he challenged her to stay focused. Jodie still had her love for salsa, and she kept her new condo filled with the sultry sounds which played in the background when her son Calvin did his homework.

Jodie had a growing career as a financial aid officer. Her job not only allowed her to help other students find ways to finance their educations, but she learned the tricks of the trade to finance her own MBA. She and Calvin did their homework together. He was a growing young man who would pursue little league and then high school baseball. Jodie encouraged him with the same hard working ethic that her own father had instilled in her.

Jodie's experiences as a financial aid officer provided a nice transition to civilian life, with her financial aid experiences. She took a position as an assistant financial aid director at a small private university in the greater Washington, DC area. Her goal was to earn promotions and stay in her position long enough for Calvin to attend tuition free in four years. With her leadership abilities and focus, Jodie earned a promotion two years later when her Director left for a bigger school. She was asked to serve as interim director; after a search for a new Director, the search committee decided unanimously that Jodie was the best person for the job. She knew the school's student population; she was well-liked, and very efficient. Jodie's first tasks were to hire an assistant, and have the financial aid office relocated to the student success corridor so her office would be more visible. She was successful in all objectives. Through her continuous meetings with operations and central administration, Jodie's financial aid department was relocated into the newly renovated building. Although students typically complain about financial aid offices, Jodie's office consistently received high marks in the student satisfaction survey. Her career was going well; her son was advancing successfully through junior high school, and she had completed her MBA. Her father and the army had taught her a great deal about forecasting and perseverance.

At the completion of her sixth year at the National College of Defense and Strategy, the president, Jodie was invited by Dr. Russell to apply for the controller's position. The president's goals included expanding the university's presence in greater Washington, DC, adding online and hybrid courses, and establishing adult learning centers to serve adult students with evening courses. He told Jodie they would need a strong financial officer to help with the transition, and guide the ethical trajectory of their financial policies. Jodie knew the school well, and had achieved noted success. Dr. Russell was sure she could help him take the school to the next level.

Jodie was encouraged by her new task. She let her dad know she was promoted and went to work on developing new revenue streams with academic affairs. In her role, Jodie also worked with development and marketing to manage the revenue streams, report to donors, and provide accountability reports for donors and the board. Jodie's work was impeccable, and was a keystone for the small private university. One day she was working with the biology chair about plans to develop a new lab. It had to be sustainable, be ADA compliant, and bring in some of the latest microscopes, lasers and training facilities. The plans were reviewed by the chair before she arrived at the meeting. When she entered the office, Jodie was surprised to see the biology chair, Dr. Martha Cameron, wiping away tears.

"I'm sorry; I am just dealing with some harsh news. I ..."

Jodie was concerned, "Take your time, I can come back."

"No, I have to go to Palo Alto next week, and then to another conference. If we don't meet now, I won't see you for a month." Martha collected herself and said, "I just can't believe Dr. Russell allowed such a thing."

Jodie's ears were perked. She didn't want to get involved, but she felt awkward not asking for more information. "What do you mean?"

"Dr. Russell's son assaulted my daughter. It happened a month ago, but she is just telling me now."

"I'm so sorry, I didn't realize…"

"No one will realize. Dr. Russell threw two years of free tuition at my daughter so she signed a waiver. She can't talk about it… and oh… I …" Martha apparently had just heard the news and realized she was talking about it.

"I can't believe I am telling you all this. Please, Jodie, please, I can't get her in any more trouble."

Jodie protested, "But why is your daughter in trouble? She..."

"I just don't want anything to come of it. Let's get on with the meeting."

Jodie wanted to ignore it, but Dr. Russell had just given away $42,000 in school resources to cover-up his son's assault. He was obviously trying to keep it out of the papers, but this would show up in her audit. Unless Dr. Cameron's daughter was a Rhodes Scholar, she couldn't justify receiving that kind of money. It was a shame Dr. Cameron had not joined the staff five years ago when there was 100% tuition remission for faculty and staff; then Dr. Russell would not have this chip to play.

Jodie was uncomfortable with this information. She spent the next two weeks contemplating ways to ignore it, or let it go. She thought of her own son, Calvin; he needed tuition in a couple years. But how could Jodie ignore the rape of a young girl, and say nothing. Her parents didn't raise her like that.

Jodie went to Human Resources to discuss the problem confidentially. She didn't use names or dates or pertinent information. But she also knew by bringing up a felony the school would be required to act on it. Throughout the meeting she tried to speak on hypothetical situations, bring up other erroneous details, but still bridge the issue. At the end of the meeting Jodie felt assured that the matter would be held with the utmost confidentiality.

With new building contracts and the holiday season coming, Jodie was busy making a final review of the school's revenue in the last six months. She reviewed athletics' money, the development revenue, and other capital expenditures. She felt a pang in her stomach when it was time to review the scholarship dollars.

Almost as if on cue, Dr. Russell knocked. "Hi Jodie," he entered, "I know you're doing a great job."

Jodie was startled, "Wanted to get this report to you before we go on winter break."

Dr. Russell sat down, "Yes, I was reviewing the numbers as well. I know you see our university took a hit this year with the clean-up from that hurricane, and then the metro accident close to campus hurt recruitment for next term. We didn't make the class. Enrollment is way down for next term."

Jodie commented, "I know, but we have that capital campaign starting up after Valentine's Day and…"

Dr. Russell was not following her. "I have prepared this letter, you will be fine, and you are very talented."

Jodie was confused, and opened the letter. It was a very generous severance package of seven months' salary plus health insurance for her and her son for a year, and a reference on the president's letterhead. Jodie wrinkled her eyebrows. "I thought you needed this position. Hey, I can always go back to being Director of Financial Aid."

"I'd have a law suit Jodie; I just hired an African-American male in that spot, and he has his doctorate. So if I fire him to put you there," he paused, "You know we don't need any more bad press." Dr. Russell continued, "I have to eliminate some positions, cut back. It will be lean here."

Jodie knew this to be true; she had made some of the other recommendations with adjuncts and a few administrators. She never thought the controller would get the ax, too. She was dying to ask how she could get cut, when Dr. Russell had just covered $40,000 in tuition dollars for his son. She never mentioned it, but she knew that trip to HR was hurting her. "I am upset with this, but…"

Dr. Russell continued, "It's a great severance package. And if we can bring you back, I will lead the way to get you rehired."

Somehow Jodie didn't believe him. She reluctantly signed the severance papers. She had good credentials. With army training and her MBA from Georgetown, she expected that she would be somewhere else by March.

Dr. Russell stood up and shook her hand. "Jodie, I wish we could keep you on. I hope you have a good holiday."

Jodie let Dr. Russell exit gracefully. She stood stunned under the fluorescent lights. She fought the growing lump in her throat still hurt by a forced separation. She turned back to her desk to re-read the severance letter she had signed:

*As of December 22, 20xx, Josephine Barstowe relinquishes her position at the National College of Defense and Strategy. The college has offered her full seven months' salary and a full year of health benefits for the separated employee and any dependents currently on her health plan. In exchange, the undersigned agrees and does hereby release from liability and agrees to indemnify and hold harmless the National College of Defense and Strategy and any of its employees or agents representing or related to the University as regard to this separation. This release is for any and all liability. By signing this document, all parties understand the terms set forth in this agreement. The undersigned further agrees to abide by all the rules and regulations promulgated by the National College of Defense and Strategy and/or its affiliate groups and vendors throughout the separation pro*cess.

Jodie paused. She sat at her desk and picked up the phone to call the president's office. She figured this was an amicable separation. Right? She called the president's office to inform them she was leaving for the evening and she would come back with Calvin after the break to collect her things.

Despite the news, Jodie had a nice winter break with Calvin. They had a few friends over for the New Year, and even had her parents up from Florida for a couple days. On the night before her parents were to leave, her father approached her.

"Jodie, you aren't yourself. Just checking in here." He sipped on a hot toddy and kicked back. "I know your mom and Calvin had a ball today at the mall…. "His voice trailed off, inviting her in.

"Well Pop, I was let go. The college let me go right before the holidays." Her dad perked up. "What happened?"

"Cut backs, tight resources, and, well, I stuck my nose in something. I couldn't help myself. I don't regret it, but, well, I got seven months' full pay and health benefits."

"Hmmm…. Sounds like an opportunity to me. You have been squawking about building your own business for years. You have that fancy MBA, military experience, and you live in one of the largest areas of military personnel. Honey, think about it. You just got your seed money."

Jodie's eyes twinkled for the first time in ten days.

Her father continued, "I have a few clients here in Washington that I have been trying to refer, but they don't trust anyone. Tax season is coming, think a minute."

"So Pop, uh, can you stick around a couple more days? I would like to bring you with me to check out a couple things. I could use your insight."

"Well, I don't know. If you fix your old man another hot toddy, I think I can throw some money to your mom for Tyson's Corner and we can make some things happen."

* * * * *

Jodie and her dad spent the next few days looking into registering a business, considering office space, and chatting with a website designer. Given her dad's experience in business, Jodie accomplished in a week what took most people six months. She didn't want new clients coming to her house with Calvin there, and found a small office about ten miles away. Her dad helped her set up, and gave her tips about being in an office alone: Lock the door after 6 pm. Have two phones, and a cell phone, and always keep the radio on; it gives the illusion of someone else in the office, even though everyone knows there is only one person. Have Calvin stop in and out and make friends with the local police and security in the building.

By the time Jodie returned to school to get her personal things after the winter break, she had already filed expedited LLC paperwork with the state, signed the lease on office space, and had a draft website up with email. She almost bounded into her old office.

"Wow," her former assistant said, "You seem awfully happy...."

Jodie smiled as Calvin whisked past her to her old office to start packing. "Well, I am finally starting that business I was talking about. I have the time now." She gave her assistant a few business cards. "It was time for me to do something about what I want to do."

The assistant smiled and eyed the card through her half-moon glasses, "Do you need office help on the weekends? I could use a little extra..."

Jodie paused, but realized with tax season she would need help, especially on weekends. "Well, Betty, give me a call. I know tax season really opens up in a couple weeks, and I could use someone at the phones."

"And maybe you could look at my taxes? I never liked doing them myself. 1040 EZ is not for me!"

"Sure, I'll look at them." Jodie was surprised at all the love here, and a bit suspicious. But she knew Betty was a strong union officer, and a good word from Betty easily meant 25 clients.

Betty continued, "I know my days might be numbered here. Things are changing."

Jodie's brow fluttered. "What do you mean?"

"Turns out Russell had another set of books. Things you couldn't have known about. He let go about ten people right before the holiday. Apparently someone called the board and tipped them off. We aren't supposed to know, but rumor is an investigation will start next week. Seems you got out just in time."

Jodie smiled to herself. Being caught up in some investigation would have been a bigger blow to her career than the forced separation.

Betty kept running her mouth, "He has been covering up stuff for years. Jodie, it was time for you to move on."

Calvin came out of the office, "Ma, I didn't see anything else really, except that corny picture of me from 5th grade."

Jodie replied, "I always did like that picture; I have a box, and I'll get the rest."

Calvin went on, "Don't want to rush you mom, but you said we could catch the Senators tonight and get pizza."

Betty looked over, "Hmm, must be the life, pro basketball, pizza, new business..."

Jodie simply turned, "You reap what you sow." She went to her old office to collect a few stray items. She reemerged in the vestibule and said, "Call me Betty; I am sure we can work things out."

"Sure, Jodie, I think you are on to something."

Chapter 5

Aliza Rojas—Interviewing in the wild wild west

Employers should adhere to well-documented and concise hiring and interviewing procedures. Under ADA (Americans with Disabilities Act) and ADEA (Age Discrimination in Employment Act), it is illegal to discriminate during the hiring process. In some states, these protections have been extended beyond the federal categories to include marital status, sexual orientation, and arrest and conviction records.

Aliza grew up outside of Cheyenne, Wyoming. The spacious landscape and snow-capped mountains provided a peaceful backdrop for her family who emigrated from Laredo, Texas. The second born of Mexican immigrants, Aliza translated for her folks who worked the land and raised a family of four children. She and her older brother were the English front line, pushing back language barriers and forging a new way for their younger brother and sister. Aliza marveled at the wide open spaces and knew there was a world out there for her, through education.

She swallowed her pride through middle school and high school, ignoring bogus questions about tacos, sombreros and burros. She couldn't stand that Spanish-speaking rat from Bugs Bunny, Speedy Gonzales "¡Andale! ¡Andale! ¡Arriba! ¡Arriba! ¡Yii-hah!" "Hello, pussy cats! You looking for a nice fat mouse for deenner?" She heard racist jokes as a weekly part of her adolescence. She wanted to fight, but her brother always advised her not to be so outspoken. No one wants some firecracker beige woman in their face telling them how to run things. Her parents never went to the kids' school; they didn't want to be highlighted as immigrants in a town still adjusting to the influx of Mexican workers.

Upon graduation, Aliza took her solid grades in math and science and went to the local Laramie County Community College. She earned a great financial aid package through the WYIN, Wyoming Investment in Nursing Program. She kept her head down here, but was able to make strides with the nursing director. She watched the other students network with the nursing faculty and mimicked the process. She convinced her cousin Marcia to join her, and together Aliza felt empowered, with support from her family. The two formed a small Mexican nursing student group. They talked about the need for bilingual training for nurses to better serve Hispanic and Chicano populations. Even with their proactive civic activities, they gained the constant respect of the nursing faculty. They were student leaders and often provided bilingual tutoring services to other students who were struggling. They made strides in their programs and were selected for internships at Cheyenne Regional Medical Center.

In two and a half years, Aliza Rojas graduated with honors. She was at the top of her class and could have continued on with Marcia at Cheyenne Regional Medical Center. Instead, she was recruited as an independent nursing contractor. Given the nursing shortage across the country, nurses were recruited to serve hospital contracts of 6-18 months all over the country. Aliza saw this as a chance to travel, network with others, and bring back those lessons to her community in Wyoming.

Her first assignment was a six month stint in Seattle, Washington, at the Seattle Children's Hospital. The large city was fast-paced compared to Wyoming, and the diversity was exciting. She was of service to more blacks, Pacific Islanders, and Hispanics. The constant rain didn't dampen her mood, as her career blossomed with the accolades she received from the charge nurse. Though she missed her cousin and the rest of her family, Aliza grew more confident in her ability to work with various people, and to show her strength in nursing. She took on a second 18-month contract in Seattle to continue her knowledge and networking.

For her third assignment, Aliza took a position at Greater Lakes Medical just outside Chicago. She was hired as part of a new trauma team to work with emergency head trauma injuries in the ER. It was a grueling and fast-paced environment. Aliza helped with triage and intake, and coordinated trauma patient and family service. Her work also included assisting doctors in approaching families for organ donor procedures. It was a slow but steady road to acceptance, but this western girl had earned the respect of doctors and staff. She even got Greater Lakes into a more sophisticated organ donor registry.

The hours were long, sometimes 48 consecutive hours. However, at 29, she had the youth and stamina to maintain the pace. She was learning valuable information and making inroads with the medical community. Just as she had made contacts in Seattle, Washington, she believed that the people and information she learned in Chicago would help her gain the knowledge necessary to write grants and establish a medical clinic for the underprivileged back in Wyoming. Her intention was to maintain her presence in a large metropolitan area, and also support Marcia with the new clinic at home. It was ambitious, almost insane, but after watching the strides her mother and father made as language minorities, she knew she could forge ahead as well. As her 18-month contract was ending, the hospital administration approached her for a 36-month appointment that could lead to a permanent position in the Career and Teaching Center. Aliza's background not only made her a good trauma nurse, it also made her a good instructor for other interns who came through the medical center. After learning the nuances of the organ donor sector, Aliza was proud to sign with Greater Lakes as part of their teaching mission in regard to trauma education. If she continued to do well, the administration would transition her in about nine months to a permanent position. However, nine months turned out to be too long.

Like many hospitals, Greater Lakes was facing budget cuts. Their maternity ward was closed, sending pregnant women an additional 25 minutes out of their way to Chicagoland Medical Complex. The orthopedic center scaled back on hip replacements and knee replacements. There was a hiring freeze for nurses, creating an even bigger strain on the already overworked trauma staff. Burnout of the nursing staff was intense. The hospital needed to keep nurses somehow. To date, Aliza had not seen the life cycle of a hospital. As she entered her third year on the same site — the longest period of time Aliza had spent in any health care environment — she saw how the shifting culture had a stressful impact on doctors, nurses, staff, and patients. With so many changes at Greater Lakes, Aliza's career path was in jeopardy as well. Many of the staff who had signed on with Aliza had been transferred to another unit in the hospital.

A new Director of Health Operations and Training was hired, with the mission of moving forward with a true Career Center, and to also streamline procedures. Director Katz seemed like a kind enough woman, in her late 30s, edgy. Though Katz was direct, and an expert in her field, it was clear that she was not trying to mentor Aliza or anyone else. Katz was a hard-core Chicago Bears fan. She grew up in the area, and planned to live and die there as well.

Within the first three weeks, Katz summoned Aliza. "I know people promised you a full-time position if you signed this 36-month contract. Your contract is a contract, so don't worry about your remaining time."

Aliza replied, "Well thanks, Ms. Katz."

"But I'm gonna post the position they promised you. I want to do a thorough job in hiring just the right person."

"Are you saying I am not the right person? You can ask around, I have great references."

"Well, Aliza," Katz's jaw locked a bit and her eyes refocused to the mild challenge, "I haven't been here six months; I need to make that determination for myself." Katz waited for Aliza through the awkward pause. "But you are welcomed to apply to the position if you like."

"Understood."

Aliza saw the challenge in her. She could call her contracting company and explain the situation. They could negotiate her out of the contract if she agreed to sit out of rotation for three months to find another assignment. But she had earned this position in Chicago; she was well-liked and had over seven years of direct experience. She had even picked up her Bachelor's degree online, obtaining an added credential not required for her role. Aliza had decided to fight for her promotion. She got letters from doctors in Seattle and Chicago. She had her portfolio of materials and a brief presentation ready to go. She even hired a career coach to help her with her resume and cover letter. Aliza applied for the position of Education Director and Intern Services, and patiently anticipated the interview.

Two months passed, and no word came through. She didn't want to press Katz, but she saw the position had closed over 5 weeks ago. She hadn't heard about interviews or meetings. It was as if the position never existed.

After ten weeks of waiting, Katz walked through the ward with a young lady, Candace Hastings. Candace, or Candi as she cooed when shaking people's hands, was barely 21. She had a tight hair style, shaved to the nape of her neck, with luxurious curls popping from the top. Candi was slender but top heavy; some of the doctors craned their necks as her bust line moved through the ward. As they approached Aliza's station, Katz's uncharacteristic toothy smile dwindled down to a wry grin.

"Aliza, meet Candi, our new Education Director for Intern Services. She is a recent graduate of Lakeside Technical School. Today is her first day."

Candi reached out her hand, "Hey, nice to meet you."

Aliza couldn't believe it. Candi still had milk on her breath, no experience. Katz had hired some malleable former student from the tech school where she teaches. Aliza didn't even get to interview for the position. Aliza had to save face, which was growing hot with disbelief and embarrassment. "Good to meet you — I am sure you will like it here. If you need anything, feel free to ask."

"Thanks. Alice, is it?"

"No, it's Aliza, with a "z"."

Candi giggled to herself. "Great."

Katz chimed in: "She was my star pupil. Great work ethic. Aliza, I know you two will be working closely together."

Katz and Candi walked off. Aliza watched them stroll away, almost like sorority sisters, almost like they were walking too close together.

* * * * * *

That night Aliza called her cousin Marcia in tears. She was distraught and working on finishing a large Chicago pizza on her own. "I can't believe it. They didn't even interview me!"

"Well Aliza, maybe it's time for you to come home. I can hear you downing some large amount of food. You will be big as a house. Stop stressing. Remember, you weren't sure you would take the next contract in Chicago."

"I'm stuck here now, for another two and a half years. And with Katz and Candi, I feel like I'm stuck in some tacky Doonesbury cartoon."

"Hey, learn what you can, and get through the two and a half years, and then come home."

Aliza felt strangled by the lump in her throat. She tried not to cry. "I know life isn't fair, but this girl knows nothing!"

Marcia chimed in, "Not your problem is it?"

"Guess not…."

But Aliza soon discovered it that it was her problem. Katz assigned Candi to shadow Aliza, to have Aliza train her. Aliza was working double time to work through her own shift, while showing Candi the set up of the ward, how to pitch in with the admission protocol, and what training materials interns used in various trauma procedures. Aliza was spending 30% of her time training Candi, and then spending what little lunch time she had to catch-up, while Candi and Katz never missed a lunch together.

Aliza remembered, hell is your own life gone wrong. Her once-chipper spirit had been trashed. She was haggard, edgy, and for the first time, homesick. She went through the motions, counting the days. About a month after the appointment, a new wave of interns came through. Melinda, the one from Lakeside Tech School, was a bit older, but glad to work in the medical field. She surveyed the place as she checked in with Aliza. Candi walked by with the little switch in her walk and turned the corner.

"Oh- so I see Kitty Katz got her Candi Cane."

Aliza looked up, "Excuse me?"

"I spoke out of turn." Melinda was embarrassed. "Did I say that?"

Aliza took interest."Yeah you said it out loud. What do you mean?"

"Don't you know those two are lovers? Candi was teacher's pet all the way through school. We hated it. She doesn't know what she's doing. I heard that Katz promised her a job when she got appointed. I didn't know that — I mean I didn't realize it had happened."

Aliza was stunned.

"Hey, and Candi will suck all the knowledge outta you just so she can get through. I don't have to work with her, do I?" Melinda realized that Aliza was in the clouds. "Didn't you know they are lovers, and practically live together? Anyway. I just want to do my six week internship and move on. I don't mean to have a bad attitude on the first day, but I gotta keep it real."

Aliza was frozen. She checked in Melinda and pointed her to admissions. Aliza stayed in some other zone the rest of the morning. In her disbelief, Aliza made a point to follow Candi at lunch. Are people that unfair? As Candi left the ward for lunch, she did walk by Katz's office slowly, never entering. A minute later, Katz exited her office to follow. During some of the renovations, parts of the hospital were under construction. Aliza walked along in the shadows of the corridor to see Katz catch Candi and squeeze her behind. Candi giggled, so silly Aliza could hear it 100 feet away.

Aliza was startled not only by the injustice, but Katz appeared to be so together. How could she allow herself to get caught on the job with her lover? The two paused. Katz kissed Candi dead on the mouth, deeply; then she pulled back her shirt to expose Candi's push up bra. They drifted behind some construction plastic and turned off all the lights in the corridor. Aliza didn't need to stick around to know for sure what happened next.

It made sense now, why she didn't even get an interview. Katz was going to hire her lover the entire time. And Candi didn't even have any credentials or experience.

Aliza mulled over this problem. Over the next week, Candi of course continued to pepper Aliza with stupid questions. Katz was smiling like the Kat who eats the Candi, and Melinda kept her head down and her mouth quiet.

A month after Candi was hired, Aliza Rojas filed an internal complaint with the hospital. She specifically stated that she was passed over for a promotion because of her race. She was not even granted an interview. Aliza provided documents of past reviews and her successful changes in her position. She spoke with a representative in HR who kindly wrote everything down and said they would look into it.

The next two weeks were tough. Katz stopped speaking to Aliza. But Aliza got a break; all of Candi's questions went to Melinda now. Aliza soon noticed that everything was going to Melinda. People stopped speaking to her. Her lunch buddies faded into the background; it became a very sterile and cold climate for Aliza.

Aliza was then summoned to Human Resources to discuss the findings of her case.

"Technically, you're not an employee of the hospital. You are a contractor from Safer Hands Contracting. Therefore, you really don't have the right to complain with this employer. You need to go to your own employer."

Aliza returned a cold stare, "Are those my only options?"

The HR representative pushed back from the desk, "I believe so. You really have to speak with your employer."

Aliza stood up and nodded. The meeting lasted all of five minutes. Upon her return she received a memo from Katz informing her that her schedule has been changed. Instead of working from 7 am – 4 pm with on call duties, she will now report from 6 pm to 3 am. Aliza was not surprised by the change. She saw it coming. Now that the findings were in from the hospital's internal investigation, Katz felt free to continue her mistreatment. However, the change to the less desirable schedule was retaliation.

Frustrated at first, Aliza embraced the daytime hours off as an opportunity. She gathered her records, pay stubs, programs, and references. She made a point to review the retaliatory and EEOC policies of both her employer and the hospital. One thing she learned growing up Mexican in Wyoming, you have to stand up for your rights.

Aliza complained to the City of Chicago Commission on Human Rights as a Mexican Chicano woman who was passed over for a white woman who had half her credentials, and was a lover of the boss. Second, she endured retaliation when she was assigned to a less desirable shift after she filed her internal complaint. Aliza maintained that she had more experience and credentials than Candi, yet she was not even granted the opportunity to interview for the position.

In 30 days, Aliza received a reply from the hospital. They denied that the position of Education Director had even been posted. The hospital stated that they were restructuring, and that hiring decisions were based on business necessity. They denied the retaliation charge saying many employees worked odd hours. However, in the three years Aliza worked there, she never had the swing shift.

Aliza was relieved that her own contracting company found a different assignment for her at the end of 12 months without making her commit to the entire 36-month contract. She did not even need to sit out. Her placement officer did mention something about, "The hospital no longer needed her." When the hospital prematurely ended the contract, Aliza endured a second retaliatory action.

The case and investigation went on despite her relocation. As a contract employee, she did not have additional contact with anyone at the hospital. She received no updates; she was just left with the hurt that she was passed over for a position she was obviously qualified for.

The Chicago Commission contacted her 18 months later to alert her to the findings. Not only was Aliza passed over, several other women were not granted interviews. While Aliza was not privy to the names and situations of the other women, her commission investigator verbally confirmed that one woman over 40 was ignored, despite the fact that she had 14 years' direct experience. No one was interviewed. Candi got the job unopposed. The investigator also quietly applauded Aliza stating that she was the only one who came forward, and that the hospital would take corrective action in their hiring practices as a result. Also, Aliza discovered that the key witness was Melinda Davis. Melinda knew of the situation that had originated from the tech school. Once Aliza relocated, Melinda called the Chicago Commission to offer her support.

Though Aliza's claim of racial discrimination was weak, the Commission supported Aliza's two charges of retaliation. It was simple. Aliza complained, then the hospital adversely changed her working conditions. Aliza was awarded six months' back pay, to cover the period from when she applied for the position, to when her company relocated her; front pay was also part of this calculation. She used the money to pay off her student loans and start a small retirement savings account.

When all was resolved, Katz remained in her position, just stripped of her hiring authority. Candi was quietly reassigned to a job that more closely met her credentials, in a hospital annex two miles away. The hospital moved forward without much consternation. But a page had been added to their employee handbook and human resources policies. Going forward, all positions must be posted for a minimum of ten business days. All applications will be carefully considered. New hires and promotions will always include the decision of the hiring authority, the hiring authority's supervisor and a third party from another division. Greater Lakes Hospital encourages all applicants, regardless of race, creed, religion or nationality.

Chapter 6

Elaina & Morgan Bradley—Half million dollar baby

The pregnancy discrimination act (PDA) was a 1978 amendment of the Title VII Civil Rights Act of 1964. Pregnancy discrimination is considered a form of sex discrimination. Under some circumstances, a pregnancy is covered by the Americans with Disabilities Act (ADA). Many laws regulate how women are to be treated if they are disabled or on bed rest during pregnancy. Similar employment issues and considerations also apply in regard to adoption.

Elaina was a 34 year old Caucasian female living in Short Hills, New Jersey. In her early 20s she was married to a great guy, Jake; but after a few years she realized that she wasn't being true to herself. She had dated a few women, calling it a trip to the mall, or going out for drinks with friends. But the kisses good night with women let her know that it was good night for her marriage as well.

Married and divorced by 29, Elaina had not let go of her dream of motherhood. Her career in education kept her in touch with kids, and she enjoyed helping them to develop. But it was not the same as having her own. She also realized that she really wanted to have a two parent household. A lesbian two parent household; should that be so difficult? She was living 45 minutes from New York City. Her family had died in a car accident, leaving her alone in her early 20s.

Elaina started looking at all her options as the days ticked by. She was pleased to find the IVF lab in Somerset, New Jersey. They could harvest her eggs and keep them in a nitro chamber until she found the right partner. The costs were $10,000 plus all the medical follow-up to watch her body as it went through this process to "grow" multiple eggs for harvest. She had saved up the money, and had some left over from her inheritance. She felt it would take the pressure off her in so many ways. Though the procedure made her nauseous and sluggish, she was relieved to have made the decision and had the procedure in the summer, before she returned to teaching in the fall.

The next school year brought the sense of promise that Elaina always welcomed. The kids at her Catholic charter school were creative, rambunctious and welcoming. Elaina had been working for the school over seven years teaching 8th grade English. She had a way of conveying *Great Expectations* and *The Good Earth* to kids who would rather play outside. For Halloween, they bobbed for apples and began their writing unit on Shakespeare. Watching the kids grow year after year, Elaina knew she had to leave her little cocoon and find her life partner. Sure, she had a few dates, a couple short term relationships, but no one she could build a life around.

Just before Thanksgiving, Elaina went with a few friends to a bar on the east side in New York. It was the same scene, except she saw someone new. Elaina could not take her eyes off Morgan, a redhead, tall, and funny. Morgan noticed Elaina too. They struck up a conversation and talked until the bar closed. Elaine told her friends to catch the last New Jersey Transit without her. Elaina and Morgan went to Morgan's apartment in the village. It was quaint and well-kept. Elaina marveled at Morgan's degrees — Dartmouth grad, Wharton MBA. Morgan was a gracious hostess. They talked all night over Irish coffee and old photos of family and friends. Elaina felt so at home.

Morning came and they went off to a diner for French toast and cocoa. Their friendship was a fast love at first sight. After breakfast Elaina realized she had not been to sleep in almost 24 hours. "I really have to go…"

Morgan was polite but made her intentions known, "I want to see you next weekend." She gave Morgan a sweet kiss, tentative, but nice.

Elaina blushed. "But we have to talk before that. Will you come to Short Hills?"

Morgan replied, "I will be there with bells on."

* * * * * *

Through the holiday season their relationship flourished. Elaina shared her own history, that she was the love child; both of her parents were nearly fifty when she was born. She only knew them until their death when she was in her mid-twenties. Morgan was a comfort, and told of her family — her coming out, how her mom still embraced her, but her brother called her some abomination. Her dad, well she would always be daddy's girl. They had the same deep blue eyes and red hair. Elaina and Morgan found themselves spending every weekend together. Chatting like girlfriends, drifting into each other's space like lovers. It was natural, like home, like family. They spent Christmas and New Year's together like it had always been that way. They were serious, without making it a big deal. But they were always together.

Morgan and Elaina made plans to move together to a bigger place in Short Hills. Morgan knew that New York was such a fast place. With the rate their relationship was developing, they were already making casual conversation about going to Massachusetts to get married, having a family, sharing their lives.

Their relationship was not without problems. Morgan wanted to visit Elaina at school, but Elaina desperately wanted to keep her personal life under cover.

"You mean you haven't come out on your job? Like they don't know."

"Morgan, trust me it is just better this way. It's a Catholic School. It's bad enough I am divorced. I have watched how they treat people."

"Don't you think sooner or later they will see us at the mall, or at dinner?"

"Well, I will deal with them when the time comes."

* * * * * *

The April after they met, Morgan left Manhattan for a Short Hills, New Jersey apartment the two had picked together. Elaina commented, "I never thought this could happen to me."

Morgan countered with a quick kiss on the cheek, "What, you thought people like us can't be happy? Like we are the scourge of the earth? Love is love; we just have to fight harder to find it sometimes."

Morgan and Elaina decorated their apartment, had friends over, and had a few dinner parties. They were living a nice life, and they were undeniably happy. Elaina confessed to her frozen eggs in Somerset. She entered the baby conversation lightly, not wanting to upset the boat. Morgan was thrilled "I should have told you, Elaina, I can't have kids. I had ovarian failure in my twenties. But wow, I could be a mom, we can be moms together."

Elaina and Morgan shopped the sperm banks for the right donor. Morgan joked, "Shame my brother thinks I am fit to be damned, his red headed sperm would have been perfect." The two investigated sperm banks' policies. Will they let the child meet the father at 18? Could they meet the father? Had the sperm led to successful pregnancies before? Was it washed, unwashed? How many units did they have to buy at once? What would this cost? There were so many questions.

The women decided on a sperm bank in New England that had a videotape of the donors. They agreed on a red head to resemble Morgan. And they liked Donor Smith; he was listed as smart, athletic, he had a bit of a lisp, and a good sense of humor. The next decision was to decide to use Elaina's frozen eggs, or the fresh ones she was still producing through regular periods. She had just turned 36, and they were still quite viable. Morgan had taken on this project with all the exacting detail of her financial strategist career. The two went to a doctor and decided the frozen eggs were the backups; they would use the freshly delivered eggs since they were available.

Then the counting began. Morgan and Elaina were tracking Elaina's ovulation down to the minute. Once they had mastered a total cycle, Morgan ordered the frozen sperm. The big day was there. Ovulating Elaina and Donor Smith will join egg and sperm to create a family for Morgan and Elaina. They followed every direction, thawing out the sperm, using the syringe for the "ejaculation" and other stimulation to get the sperm to move to the egg. Elaina and Morgan shared a glass of Elaina's favorite white wine to relax her. When their baby making was over, Morgan held Elaina and patted her stomach.

Two weeks later Morgan found Elaina weeping in the bathroom over a pregnancy test. Elaina was teary eyed "I thought we had done it. I just knew since we had been planning." The pregnancy wand displayed the obnoxious negative sign. Elaina held it up. "Not Pregnant." Morgan inspected the wand.

"Elaina, did you think it would happen the first time? Even with natural couples under 30, they have a 1 in 5 chance."

"How do you know all this, Morgan?"

"I want this baby as much as you do. I have been reading up. We will keep tracking your ovulation and try again."

Elaina felt herself blessed to have such a supportive and smart partner. With an unsteady sigh, she stood up from the bathroom floor.

Two months, three attempts, and $2000 in sperm bank costs later, Morgan and Elaina were finally pregnant. Elaina was ecstatic. Morgan, the logical one, had already investigated obstetricians, prenatal yoga, and a nutritionist. "Elaina, you are gonna have such a healthy pregnancy. This is gonna be hard, but we are doing this together."

At first, Elaina slept constantly. She was exhausted at work that fall. She couldn't have coffee or colas. She made a point to stay on her feet so she didn't doze off in front of her students. Morgan packed her lunches with Greek yogurt, nuts, and roast beef sandwiches. Elaina could just hear her voice, "Brain food for the baby — red meat!"

The weeks passed. Week 5, week 6, week 7. At week 8 they heard the baby's heartbeat. Morgan and Elaina cried when they saw the ultrasound. Elaina had never been so excited, coming into the holiday season, pregnant and full of joy.

"So, Elaina, did you tell that stodgy school of yours yet that you need FMLA?"

"Ah, no... I wanted to get through the first trimester."

"Okay Elaina, I get that, but you have to tell, we have to be ready for all this."

Elaina nodded, "I'll tell after the holiday that will be week 15. I got this, Morgan."

"Ok, don't make me come down to that school and out you!"

They laughed, and held up the ultrasound image of their baby.

* * * * *

Elaina remained active during her pregnancy. She and Morgan kept up their routine at the gym. Morgan had signed her up for yoga on days Morgan had to work late in the city. Her second prenatal appointment went well, at week 12. There was a bit of spotting; but it was so faint Elaina didn't even mention it to Morgan. The ultrasound was normal; her weight gain was normal. The Greek yogurt and roast beef sandwiches must have been doing some good. Elaina was happy that winter was coming. She blamed her pudgy cheeks on winter weight and wore more layers in the early winter that hit the Northeast.

In early December, Morgan dropped Elaina off at school, given the ice storm the night before. She kissed her goodbye and reminded her to catch a cab on the way home. Elaina dutifully nodded. Morgan was no sooner around the corner than Elaina was lifted by an ice slick. She fell right on her side. Some of the kids were coming in to school too. They rushed to help her. After they realized she was ok, they giggled a bit, but offered to carry her things to her desk. Elaina's pride was more hurt than anything else. The cold air covered her embarrassed blushing face. As the day went on, Elaina began to ache; she figured she had hit her back hard. She dare not take an aspirin, Aleve or anything. Her doctor said it was fine, but she risked nothing, not even second hand smoke.

After her taxi ride home, she bypassed dinner and went to soak in the bath. She was startled that her back side was all black and blue, and she was startled by the increasing blood in her panties. She did bruise easily. She felt so stupid. She was actually glad Morgan was not there to dote on her. After her bath she had herbal tea and went straight to bed.

Around 10 pm, she heard the door of the bedroom open; it was Morgan coming in from work. "Sorry I'm late," Morgan leaned in to kiss Elaina, who winced at the touch, and "I know my hands are cold Sweetie, but you have all these bed clothes on."

Elaina turned over. "I'm just not feeling well. I should be better in the morning. Will you pack my lunch again?"

Morgan smiled and left the room. She was worried, but she figured pregnancies can be so unpredictable.

The next morning Elaina was moving in slow motion. Not only did she have back pain, she also had cramping and an upset stomach. Morgan asked, "Why don't you stay home? You haven't taken a sick day yet."

"I can't. I have three birthdays to celebrate today and we have achievement tests. I'll just sit most of the day."

"Well if you don't snap out of it, I'm calling Dr. Rooney. I'm worried about you."

Elaina paused with a cramp, "Yeah this woman stuff is no picnic. Sometimes I wish you could carry the baby, even for a couple hours."

Morgan replied, "I can't even envy you. Ok, I made you oatmeal. ; I'll drive you to work and I'll get you early today. I can leave early and bring home some work."

Elaina's day went from bad to worse. The smell of the buttercream cake in the lunch room made her nauseous. For some reason, all the teachers were asking her if she had the flu. Elaina was white as a sheet. She should have listened to Morgan and taken the day off.

Just after lunch Elaina had to give the achievement tests. She had hoped that her mood would not dampen the spirits of the kids before such a big test. Her cramping was worse. She would call Dr. Rooney on break; her spotting had gotten worse over the day, too, but nothing a panty liner couldn't handle.

In front of the room, she assured the students that all was well. She told them she had eaten bad sushi the night before. They smiled, but were concerned.

"Now if you open your booklets to page 2, you will see where to...."

Elaina felt a huge rush in her pants, as if she had just gone to the bathroom. She saw blood on the floor and heard the girl in the front row gasp. That's all she could remember.   What seemed like a lifetime was 20 minutes. She woke up in the ambulance with her assistant principal holding her hand. "Elaina, Elaina..."

Elaina heard the sirens, and she only wanted Morgan.

"Elaina..."

"Call Morgan, Morgan..." Elaina's voice drifted.

Tracy Weggens, the assistant principal, was trying to talk to Elaina. "Honey, did you know you were pregnant?"

Elaina heard the EMT talk into the radio… "38 year old white female, apparent miscarriage, ETA 6 minutes."

Elaina's eyes welled up "No, what do you mean was….?" She started crying.

Tracy Weggens continued, "I'm sorry. I think you had a miscarriage. You passed all this blood standing in front of the class. One of your students ran to the office to tell us you were on the floor. We had to send your class home."

Elaina couldn't see. Her tears clouded everything. She only heard the siren, and "Call Morgan! Call Morgan." Then she passed out.

When Elaina came to consciousness again, she was holding Morgan's hand in the hospital. Morgan was always the strong one. "Elaina, babe, you gave us quite a scare."

"Morgan? Morgan!"

"I'm here. Tracy called me. They found your cell phone with your ICE number in it."

"The baby…"

Morgan paused. Tears were on her face and she was quiet.

"Morgan, tell me. Morgan…"

"You had a miscarriage, Honey. You passed a clot the size of an orange in front of the class, along with a pint of blood. They did a D&C when you came in and…

"Morgan…"

"Our baby is gone. But we can try again. This happens to a lot of women."

Elaina was sobbing by now. "How do you know so damn much?'

Crying with her, Morgan said, "You know, silly, I read a lot. Once your body settles and your hormones settle, we can try again in the new year. I'll call your school and tell them you will be out a week. I'll take care of you." Morgan was crying, too. She made room next to Elaina in the hospital bed, under the IV. "We will try again next year if you are up to it." They cried together, sobbing at their loss. There was nothing else but the snowflakes calmly falling outside Elaina's hospital window. Morgan stayed with Elaina through the night. The scary part was over.

Later that week Morgan brought Elaina her favorite Holland tulips to brighten the room. "You know how hard these are to find in December?" They shared a giggle. "You know your principal is a real dick."

"Told you..."

"No, Elaina. I mean in a legal way. I told him you would be out for a week. He didn't ask how you were doing. He didn't ask about me."

Elaina broke in, "He doesn't know you Morgan."

"Yeah, a problem I mentioned before. This nut says he will deal with you when you return. I tell him that you had a miscarriage, and he says 'how can he grant medical leave for pregnancy when you never told them you were pregnant. How can he anticipate anything like that, you aren't even married; it's a bedroom community.'"

"He said that?"

"AND! He said he was so disappointed. The school was in shock witnessing the whole thing. The afternoon was just plain unnatural."

"WHAT?!"

"Hey Elaina, I don't want to upset you; but, well, we'll talk after you get back on the job."

Elaina returned to her job ten days after her miscarriage. She was ashamed, and hurt. And she was sorry that her students saw the whole thing. As she walked up to the school, one of the parents approached her.

"Ms. Elaina, Ms. Elaina," Elaina was so scared. "Ms. Elaina, I am Karen Parker, my son Cameron is your class. I just want to say…"

Elaina's eyes were big. She knew she had traumatized the kids, herself, and the school.

"I want to say it happened to me the first time. It will be ok. You and your husband can try again."

Elaina gave Mrs. Parker a squeeze. "Thanks, I appreciate that."

Once in the building, Elaina walked slowly, not wanting to bring any attention to herself. She heard a strong voice, her principal, "Elaina, how are you?"

She turned, and blushed. All that blood, the clot, all over the floor, she was ashamed.

The principal continued, "Let's talk at the end of the day."

At day's end, Elaina reported to the principal. Her class had been nice; they had a card waiting for her. They didn't pepper her with questions about what had happened, or about all the blood. She had some real angels in her class. If only this attitude had translated to her visit with the principal.

"I am really troubled here, Elaina. Why didn't you tell us you were pregnant?"

"I ah… I didn't want you to judge me..."

"But we were going to realize it sometime."

"I know, I had talked it over with Morgan. I planned to tell you after the holidays."

"Oh Morgan," the principal said with some relief. "Your husband?"

"Ah no, Morgan is my partner. We... she and I are together."

"Oh I see. Well," the principal paused, "I talked with legal, and well, we are a Catholic organization. This whole thing was entirely unnatural, out of control. You traumatized the kids. You had a deleterious effect on the school during achievement tests. This is not the type of environment we find good for our kids."

Elaina could not believe what she was hearing.

"And, well, this other information…Morgan, I," the principal tread lightly, "In short, in light of everything, I have to ask you to give up your class."

"Are you..."

At the archdiocese, we all think this is best. You people...

"You people?"

"Elaina, this isn't easy, you are well-liked. But I am sure parents will complain. Some of the kids already had to go to counseling after witnessing such... I think this is best too. If it's any consolation, you do get to collect unemployment. Maybe give you more time to heal. Do you have a lot of personal items in your class room?"

All Elaina could think was "Wait until Morgan hears about this."

Elaina was fortunate. She didn't have to worry about money, as Morgan earned a solid six figure income. Elaina would miss teaching, but she was more upset about the indictment. She almost felt as if she was being punished for trying to start a family. Morgan was prompt in picking her up. She had NPR going, and some Chinese food she'd picked up for their dinner. Elaina was pleased to see her.

"Figured Mr. Chang's would be a nice break. I got you General Tso's chicken."

Elaina calmly got in and kissed Morgan.

"So babe, how was your first day back?"

Elaina paused, like she was waiting for a loud dog to start barking. "It was my last."

Elaina's response didn't quite register. "Come again Elaina?"

"Morgan, they let me go; said they didn't know I was married, said it was unnatural, that parents would complain."

Morgan stopped her SUV short. "WHAT?!You mean?!" She couldn't even finish her sentence. "I knew it! Goddammit!"

They drove the last 20 minutes home in silence. Elaina was tired. Her body had been through a lot. Her career was in shambles. She was relieved to let Morgan take up the mantle. When they pulled in the drive at home, Morgan marched straight for the house. She picked up her Franklin Planner, and flipped through it furiously. Elaina simply ambled behind her, gathering Morgan's briefcase and the Chinese food, walking in the front door that Morgan had left open. She heard her on the phone already: "Danny Simmons. Yeah. Hmm, I'll leave my number. Tell him to please call when he gets out of court."

Elaina just looked at Morgan. It seemed her hair was redder and her eyes a sharper blue.

Morgan continued, "You know we're not taking this lying down. Something told me that ass, your boss, argh. We can get Ivy League degrees. Make boatloads of money. It just never changes." Morgan was pacing, and then threw her cashmere overcoat across the couch.

Halfway through their silent Chinese dinner, the phone rang. "Yea, Danny…yeah…thanks for getting back to me so quickly."

Danny Simmons was a close friend of Morgan's from Penn. He was a discrimination attorney, and a good one. Elaina met him at the Christmas party last year. He had sent a card to them when he heard of the pregnancy. He was good people.

"So, the bottom fell out today…yeah, you were right. Uh huh... uh huh. I gotta talk to Elaina, but she knows we gotta fight. Uh huh…yeah... No, I don't want to screw around with some commission. I want to take it straight to 'em. I can't believe these Neanderthals still treat people like this these days." Morgan turned to Elaina, "Babe, will you feel up to going to the city to meet with Danny on Friday? We can take in a show too if you like."

Elaina nodded, happy to let Morgan be her knight in shining armor.

Morgan returned to the phone. "Yeah Danny, Friday at 2 pm. We'll be there. Thanks." During the drive to see Danny on Friday, Morgan couldn't stop speed talking. "I am just so upset about this! I can't believe this shit happens. You know, Danny has always been a fair guy. We throw each other some work sometimes. I know last year, he got some settlement for nearly a million on some ADA case dealing with access to a sporting facility. He's good people. Penn seems so far away..."

Morgan's voice droned on as she drove through the Lincoln Tunnel into midtown. Elaina's life felt like a dream, hazy. Once she was so happy, expecting a child in April. Now she is about to enter a messy employment discrimination case. The only true thing was Morgan. Speed talking, hot headed, loving and supportive Morgan.

Danny Simmons greeted them in the lobby personally. Elaina got her face together, and walked in confidently like Morgan deserved and expected. The three of them sat in Danny's office overlooking the Hudson. He took their coats, offered coffee, and then settled in with his legal pad to take notes.

Elaina became direct, no longer letting Morgan play caretaker. She stated that she was gay, and that it was her choice to be with Morgan and to be pregnant. She told of her seven years of service to the Catholic charter school and even brought the card from parents, the one she received on the last day. She had to relive the story of the miscarriage, the trip to the hospital with Tracy Weggins and the leave that she was denied. Elaina had taken notes of the things the principal had told Morgan, and the obnoxious and "unnatural" things he told her when he fired her.

Danny leaned in, eyes focused like lasers. "Well, this appears to be a Title VII discrimination case based on your pregnancy.

"But I'm not pregnant."

"Your miscarriage is covered under this. You have reproductive rights. Even if you had an abortion and they fired you for it, there would be a violation of Title VII. I'll take the case. I think you have been through so much. Send me documents with correctly spelled names, and with accurate dates. No errors." Danny paused. "I'll let you two talk it over this weekend and let me know."

Elaina cut him off, "Morgan and I already talked. Let's move on this. I am hurt, sure, and healing, but there is no reason to wait." Morgan smiled at Elaina's determination.

Elaina continued, "It was humiliating enough for this to happen at all, and then happen in front of students. But now I am fired because I want a life and a family. I read up on the website, if I go with the EEOC, sure, it won't cost us, there would be no attorney fees, but it drags out. I read that sometimes an organization settles for a pittance because they find the EEOC annoying. Others just don't respect them, and then never respond until you get a Right to Sue Letter a year and change later; therefore, leaving you to go to the attorney anyway." Elaina paused and continued.

"Morgan trusts you, so I trust you. Why wait the year for the right to sue. I think I have a right in this moment, right now! I want to sue."

The room lay silent for a moment. Even Morgan paused and then sighed.

"Ok then, I will draft a demand letter and send it to you for approval. Once they receive it, they have 30 days to respond. I'll need a copy of your medical records, and the care you received." Danny paused, "Why didn't you tell them you were 18 weeks pregnant?"

Elaina' fervor subsided somewhat, "I didn't want to answer all kinds of questions about being gay, about marriage, about how I got pregnant. I was trying to put it off as long as possible."

Danny took notes furiously — Hosss...tiile... Envii- ron- MENT —
"OK then, watch your email. I will send you an amended retainer agreement
taking the case on contingency. We will get rolling on this."

Morgan stood to shake Danny's hand, and Elaina stood as well. Morgan
commented, "Good to see you Dan, never thought..."

Danny cut her off, "We never think it can happen to us. Gotta go, have a
conference call at 4:30pm."

The case evolved as Danny Simmons described. First, the demand
letter. After 30 days, the school district said nothing except that they have
an anti discrimination policy, therefore the principal could not have acted
with malicious and discriminatory intent. Danny then moved to file a case in
Federal District court in early February. This time the district had to respond
to the court, addressing why Elaina was let go.

Elaina fielded an endless stream of request for documents. She relinquished her
medical records going back five years. The school already had all her employment
records. She had to divulge when she and Morgan "married" and moved in
together, and began sharing health insurance and car insurance together.

Next Danny reported to her on several short court appearances. The judge
seemed lukewarm on the issue of gays and marriage; however, Danny reported
the judge was visibly moved when he told the story of Elaina miscarrying in
front of 25 students.

Elaina continued to look for work, but also remained calm and cautious
as she and Morgan prepared for their family. Elaina was meditating to keep
her blood pressure low; the stress of the case and constant phone calls and
requests took a toll. Elaina was grinding her teeth in her sleep again. She
felt more like she was going into a coma every night instead of into restful
REM sleep. Morgan urged her to settle down, relax; Morgan did make enough
money for both of them. They cut out vacations, trips to Trader Joe's, and
visits to their favorite restaurants. They cut their premium TV package and
cell phone packages. Elaina shopped with coupons and they made trips all
at once to save gas. Morgan took public transportation three days a week to
work in the City.

As they cut back with their loss of income, Morgan and Elaina still got on with life. After their St. Patrick's Day party, they started tracking ovulation and conducted their baby making ceremony. Elaina was concerned at first. She felt her health was wrecked, but relaxed seeing that she already did have a family in Morgan. With her support, they were pregnant again by July 4th.

In early summer, Danny engaged in the discovery process. Elaina needed to gather lists of names, exhibits that could be used in trial. She met with Danny via phone every other week to stay abreast of what was going on. Morgan was always in conference. Danny reported that the school's attorney was a staunch conservative, and had a definite bias regarding gays and "out of wedlock pregnancies." Danny intended to exploit that bias and have the school look even more discriminatory.

"When is my deposition?" Elaina asked in late July.

Danny replied, "We actually had two near misses. I was trying to move on this in June, but the principal had some kind of surgery and asked to delay. Then a week ago, their attorney had a death in the family, and his entire calendar was pushed back. It is tough bringing together all these parties, but we are marching through; this gives us more time to prepare."

Elaina and Morgan were elated with their second pregnancy, but were very quiet about it. As a 38 year old first time mom-to-be, Elaina took an online degree during her pregnancy. She stayed up-to-date on her case and was pleased to have other projects to focus on. Morgan was just as insistent and involved as ever, taking her to the prenatal appointments, Lamaze classes, and shuttling her around to make sure this pregnancy went fine.

Fall rolled around, mid-October in fact, before all the players in Elaina's case seemed to be in full attention. It had almost been a year since she had been terminated. Time kept slipping away. With the holidays coming, and additional requests for deposing various witnesses, the case would not get on the calendar until late February or early March of the following year.

Just after the New Year, Danny stopped by to review some papers. Their court date was set for March 5. Elaina, determined as ever, waddled in, seven months pregnant. She had a rosy blush, almost angelic, with her chubby cheeks and curly hair, like some poster child for baby formula, or maternity clothes. And she was huge. Danny's eyes popped.

"I didn't .Why didn't you tell me?"

Morgan, so protective, chimed in as Elaina eased herself down into a chair, "We wanted to be sure. That miscarriage was so hard on both of us."

Danny's bewildered look transformed to triumph. "Elaina, do you have some maternity clothes, some that really show off that big belly?"

Elaina was puzzled.

"I have to update your file, I see you are committed to motherhood, and a picture is worth a thousand words."

Morgan got the thought. "Who wants a rosy, cheeky, hormonal pregnant woman on the stand? Elaina was credible without being pregnant. But get a few women on that jury, even one who had a miscarriage or knew someone who had a miscarriage, the school would be on the run."

Danny continued, "We all know these things don't usually see the inside of a court room, but this sweetens the deal." Elaina got the point. She changed to some woolen pants and a pretty red sweater that barely covered her huge seven month belly. She put on makeup and eye liner. Morgan commented that she was absolutely beautiful.

Danny snapped the photo for the file and continued to prepare them for the case. They reviewed the time line, the notice, and the medical. "You know, they are going to want to nail you for not disclosing. They will say you should have told them."

Elaina nodded, "But my being fired confirms why I was afraid to tell."

Danny smiled. "Riiightt!"

Dusk ebbed into evening. Danny felt confident, and said he would call in a week.

* * * * *

Elaina became nervous with everything going on. Her blood pressure shot up; she had dizzy spells and was soon restricted to bed rest. Her doctor even said, "Your lawsuit will have to wait." Elaina was destined to spend the last two months on bed rest, blessed that Morgan did not complain.

The Lord blesses fools and babies. Three days before the trial, Danny called. "They want to settle, no trial. Their opening number is two years' pay."

Elaina was so relieved. She and Morgan were playing their own game of chicken. They agreed between themselves to stop the case when they discovered Elaina needed bed rest. Elaina was prepared to be deposed on video or any way her doctor might approve. But she wouldn't risk a medical crisis with the emotional stress of getting on the stand.

Danny continued, "I think I can get more; there is pain and suffering, humiliation, job loss. I will keep you posted. But we got 'em!"

For the next two weeks the settlement negotiations continued on the phone. Salaries, medical costs, career, references. All of these variables were dashed around like pieces of a puzzle. But the lost pay was always two years or more, which was the stipulation to stop the court proceedings.

Elaina was relieved to do this all from home. She was lucky. She knew from research that typically there are several depositions, inquiries, etc. Danny commented that no one wanted to victimize a beautiful and pregnant woman. It was a vicious process.

The final settlement came through in early April, a full 18 months after the termination, and over a year after the case was filed. Elaina was awarded $112, 500 in lost wages, which was two and a half years' salary. She was awarded $90,000 for pain and suffering. The miscarriage was compelling. Danny argued that the hostile environment, which culminated in the termination, was a contributing factor to her miscarriage. Her medical records supported blood pressure issues, the conversation with the obstetrician on the timing of telling her boss, and the general fear she had regarding her pregnancy at the school. This school served young families, with young mothers. They could alienate their client base, good paying clients who valued life and motherhood. Though a charter school, they were affiliated with the Catholic Church, and the church had enough problems.

Just after Easter, Elaina gave birth to a 7-pound baby boy, a carrot-topped baby they named Curtis. He was perfect in every way. All the pain, spit up, cramps, weight gain, all worth it. Even the lawsuit, she would do it all again to get to this point, to hold little Curtis.

When Curtis turned three months old, Danny came over with some toys. He also brought the settlement agreement for them to look over. "Like I said, a picture is worth a thousand words." Danny picked up Curtis.

Morgan cautions, "careful he..."

Too late, Curtis burped up formula on Danny's silk tie. "That's all right. Hazards of the trade. But here it is," he said, handing the documents to Elaina.

"But how did you...?"

"I had your picture clipped on the outside of your file. I left it out in clear view when we met with the judge and when I traveled to their law offices. I had remarked that you were a determined mother." Danny paused. "I could hear their wheels turning when they saw it."

Elaina opened the letter. Surprised. "You're telling me we will net just over $200,000?"

"Yes. The last thing the Catholic Church wants is to be regarded as anti-family. Even toward a lesbian family. We are in greater New York; you have a great work record. They didn't want this."

Morgan hugged Danny. "Glad that Ivy League degree paid off!"

"Yours or mine?" Danny joked. "Elaina, as soon as you and Morgan review that and get me a signed copy, we can go ahead and make arrangements for the payment."

Elaina never thought she would have a million dollar baby. And her career would never be the same. She and Morgan had one more child using the frozen eggs in Somerset. They named their second son Danny; he too was a carrot top.

Chapter 7

Valencia Jones—Systemic racism, do the math

There is a three part consideration to establish disparate impact, meaning a particular employment practice adversely affecting a class protected under Title VII. Typically, an employee makes such cause showing statistical evidence where one class has systemically endured adverse consequence with an employer. If the employer challenges the evidence, often the employer might claim "business necessity" meaning the employer has a business-justified rationale for engaging in a practice that systematically and adversely affects a protected class in its organization. If the employer can establish "business necessity," the complainant can still make a substantial case by claiming the employer did not consider or establish a modified practice to avoid such an adverse impact on the protected class. Consequently, an employer would have to establish that there was absolutely no other reasonable way to proceed in business without adversely affecting the protected class.

Dr. Valencia Jones was a product of East St. Louis, Illinois, one of the more blighted communities in the nation. It had a checkered history, producing greats like Josephine Baker who escaped the race riots of 1917. Miles Davis grew up in East St. Louis. Olympic great Jackie Joyner Kersee came up there, as did Reginald Hudlin, the well-known African American director.

Val was from the graduate school of hard knocks. East St. Louis used to be a booming town in the 1950s, but when the railroad industry shifted, and meat packing industries left the area, it was wracked by waning industrialism and the unemployment that followed. East St. Louis, now dotted with abandoned and boarded-up buildings, began to yield block after block of disenfranchised families, streets, and whole neighborhoods. Gang violence ensued, with the Black Egyptians and War Lords bringing a twisted stability to young people who could not find comfort at home in the midst of deteriorating families, missing fathers, and overworked mothers.

Escaping one of the highest crime rates in the country, Val crossed the river to attend college in St. Louis, Missouri. She had left behind one of the only intact families in her neighborhood. Unemployed, but together, her parents urged her to move on and find her way through education. Attending the University of Missouri, St. Louis, Val was motivated by the scholarship and the promise of never returning across that river. She soon impressed her professors with her straightforward and analytical writing style. She obtained a Resident Assistant job to pay her room and board. Val also won a national scholarship in statistics and math.

Val was a no-nonsense student, only about 5'3" but a powerhouse. She kept her hair short, in a natural, because it didn't cost money for braids or a perm. Everything had a purpose, a plan. Graduating *Magna Cum Laude*, Val didn't want to stray too far from her folks. Her dad had contracted an asbestos-airborne cancer, and her mom had her hands full with his care and keeping up with her brother, Raul; he was a special needs child who struggled with developmental problems. The hospital made some medical errors in delivery, at his birth, now Raul has a settlement for life which helps pay a majority of the bills for Val's family. Her folks were OK and together, which gave her a better start than most of the kids she grew up with.

She won a graduate fellowship at Washington University in math and statistics. Her residence life experience in college landed her a Resident Assistant position there, too. Val was on her way. She had scraped through a rough beginning with great parents, who stayed over-extended. Her college career laid the foundation to graduate school and to earning her doctorate.

At 27, Val had wrapped up her studies and felt thankful to have made a way for herself. Her parents and Raul attended her graduation ceremony.

They looked so proud. In walking across that stage, Dr. Jones felt compelled to look for work close to home, looking for a teaching position in St. Louis. She could have taken one of several tenure track offers on the east coast, but she wanted to give back to the community. To everyone's surprise, she took a full-time teaching position at Gateway Community College just outside St. Louis. When asked about her choice, she told her mom "to whom much is given, much is expected."

Dr. Valencia Jones became a fixture at GCC. She organized developmental math programs for students. She became a member of the faculty senate. Her strides as a young professional were recognized as she became a union official, and a member of the Achieve the Dream Task Force. Students sought out math when she was teaching it. She had found her calling, and she was making the most out of the intellectual gifts given her.

After Val had been on campus for four years, the chair of the math department, Dr. Morris, announced his resignation. He was a well-liked gentleman who was committed to developmental education. His own life had been tough, growing up Irish Catholic on the south side of Chicago. Math, aside from God, was the only right thing. It is right or wrong, there are no maybes in math. It was exact, it was true, and it was something he knew kids needed to move into other disciplines like engineering, economic, and psychology. Dr. Morris seldom found someone else with a similar passion for helping the disenfranchised, until he met Dr. Val Jones. Though she had only been at GCC for 4 years, she was well liked, respected, and had made a significant impact on the math department. She had a successful grant from the state to start a developmental math program, and even set up a math exchange with both of her alma maters, Washington University and University of Missouri, St. Louis.

At his retirement party, Dr. Morris made a toast to his colleagues, long-standing friends, and new faculty. He had worked at GCC since its opening in 1969; he had been the chair twice during his tenure, and now he found it was time to pass along the torch, "to those with more energy."

"I have to ask Val to move on." The faculty broke into smiles, not a sour tone in the bunch. Dr. Morris continued, "Dr. Val, I know you are modest in your strength and commitment, so forgive me for taking a poll of the faculty behind your back, but I suspect you would turn me down modestly if I asked you in private. We are all asking you to chair the department. You have shown so much dedication to our traditional and non-traditional learners. You are the type of faculty GCC needs."

Val simply smiled as she watched her colleagues around the room raise their styrofoam cups and toast her with red Kool-Aid and ginger ale.

Dr. Morris continued, "And the dean has already approved it." He smiled and raised his cup too.

Val nodded her head and raised her cup. "I am really honored to be put forward. I will always do my best for the students and for my math faculty."

* * * * * *

And that was the start of Val's career in higher education administration. She continued to be a humble and committed servant. When her grant ran out from the state to support the developmental math lab, she brought along junior faculty. Together they wrote a national grant and earned twice as much money for the department. She mentored several faculty and also was a dutiful, sometimes controversial member of the union. While she was administration, she was pro-faculty, fighting for additional pay for summer school hours, requirements for sabbaticals, and financial support for community service projects. Sure, she was hated by some, but respected by many more, regardless of department.

By 40, Dr. Val Jones was a full professor with 13 years of full-time service. She had nurtured the department. Her creative pedagogy helped students 'get it' in math. Her Vice President, Dr. Swinsen, had always admired and recognized Val's work and appointed her to several committees. Soon, Val was taking on more administrative duties, and helping to review tenure decisions across all departments in the liberal arts. She was assigned some accreditation duties and emerged as the liaison from GCC to the Higher Learning Commission of the North Central Association of Colleges and Schools. Once a semester, Dr. Val was traveling to Chicago for meetings to represent GCC.

Her math faculty was not surprised when Dr. Swinsen appointed Val to the position of Assistant Vice President of Academic Affairs at GCC. Like most community colleges near urban areas, their enrollment was sky rocketing. Students who used to go straight to four-year universities were coming to the community college to do their first two years. Also, with the economy shifting, many adults were coming to school for retraining. Val seemed to understand both populations.

Val was a stellar representative for GCC. At 46, she had ascended to Assistant Vice President, remained the liaison to accreditation, and helped guide the academic trajectory of the college. To her joy, she still taught at least one night section of developmental math. Her career was good. Her life was uncomplicated, as she never married. She helped her mom with Raul from time to time. And she made a point to visit her father's grave once a term, since he had died three years before from cancer. Dr. Swinsen was more than pleased. They co-authored several articles on developmental and adult education. Dr. Val became a member of American Association of Community Colleges (AACC), and a regional representative for community colleges in the Midwest. When Dr. Swinsen announced that she was leaving for a big community college system in Texas, Dr. Val was unquestionably promoted to Vice President of Academic Affairs under college President Dr. White.

As she settled into her new role, she kept in touch with Dr. Swinsen in Texas. The transition seemed natural. The faculty was always in support of Val. She was a hometown girl who "done good" in a community where bright stars left the city instead of shining in them. The students felt supported, and all was well with the union and their accreditation.

One morning on her drive in, Val heard the local radio, "And the GCC community is still in shock to hear of the sudden death of their President Dr. White, who died suddenly of a massive heart attack at 5 am at St. Luke's Hospital. We will have more as news come forward."

Val turned the corner; the building was flanked with a few news vans beaming the news with their satellite dishes. She dodged inside, as she was not going to get caught making any statements to the press. Even at this early hour of 7:30 am, many of the President's cabinet were in, or just hearing the news on the radio. Public relations had not informed anyone.

At 9 am, Dr. Val, Vice President of Academic Affairs, the highest ranking administrator, called a cabinet meeting to discuss next steps.

With a somber voice, she said to her colleagues, "I too was saddened to learn of Dr. White's sudden passing. I have asked Marsha in public relations to send condolences, flowers and catered food to Dr. White's family. I will pass around a card if you would like to sign it." The meeting had a heavy tone to it as Val continued. She was relieved that she had earned the respect of her colleagues over the years; she felt she was talking to friends of the family, not stuffy vice presidents. They had indeed built a close-knit group. "We will cancel classes on the day of Dr. White's funeral so anyone can attend, and greet the family. We will get through this like the family we are." Dr. Val hugged a few of the Vice Presidents on their way out. The meeting was adjourned.

The next few days were hectic with press releases, statements, and getting the campus ready to mourn Dr. White. Though he was to be buried in a large Catholic cemetery downtown, he was once a state congressman, had sat on the board of TWA, and had a laundry list of friends, politics, and media who would wish to pay their last respects. Dr. Leonard White, father, civic leader, and friend, was dead at 61.

Once the media crush died down, Dr. Valencia Jones, by default, ended her term as interim president of GCC. She was to serve while the board conducted a national search for Dr. White's replacement. Val made a point to straighten up the campus functions. She continued on with her accreditation duties, worked with development and marketing to further their fund raising, and to keep their presence constant in the region. She also served in a critical role with three other Vice Presidents to choose the seventh president of GCC.

* * * * *

On July 1, Dr. Martin Hayes was installed as the seventh president of Gateway Community College. He had served in the California Community College system, and with a large community college in New York. His track record with urban populations and adult learners was evident. He was highly recommended and eagerly anticipated. Dr. Val was pleased. Dr. Hayes' inauguration brought a much-needed sense of pageantry to campus. Not only did the Board and Vice Presidents walk in the processional, civic leaders and student representatives were also embraced. It was a time to heal the campus after its shocking loss. Dr. Val sat in the front row next to an AACC colleague who was invited to give a presentation. As Dr. Hayes wrapped up his last words, Dr. Val stood up to express her enthusiasm and her colleagues followed.

The AACC organizational development chairperson smiled, "I remember you, Val, from our meetings. You have done an excellent job here at GCC, under tremendous pressure." Val smiled as the AACC colleague continued, handing Val her card. "I like you. I don't do this a lot." The colleague nodded her head in Dr. Hayes' direction. "Remember all that glitters is not gold…"

Before Val could get clarification, applause for Dr. Hayes rang across the auditorium. The members of the processional rose. Val took the business card and nodded, then turned to lead the processional from the building. Unfortunately, the AACC representative didn't stay for the inauguration party.

* * * * *

The cabinet quickly noticed static between Dr. Val and the new President Dr. Martin Hayes, or Dr. Marty. If she said up, he countered and said down. When she was quiet, he insisted she speak. When she spoke, he told her she talked too much. The Cabinet was concerned about the verbal volleyball in meetings, but soon had their hands full with Dr. Marty in their respective areas.

Dr. Marty wanted immediate changes in the public relations department. He thought their overspending was reckless, and that they had too many staff on board. The student affairs area was downsized, eliminating three sports teams, four student organizations, and minimizing the counseling area. In Dr. Val's department, tenure requirements became more stringent, with more focus on publishing and less on teaching. Dr. Val couldn't help but stand up for students and their access to proper support.

Under Dr. Marty, a campus which once bragged of diversity and over 75 faculty of color soon lost ranks among blacks and Hispanics. The budget cuts hit other areas disproportionately. Student affairs lost 10 ten staffers of color; development and Human Resources both faced the departure of a disproportionate number of blacks and Hispanics. They were the last hired, or the least qualified. When the budget was hit, they tended to be the ones to go.

Dr. Val saw the systemic problem. GCC was returning to a period when it served mostly suburban white and traditionally aged students. Their enrollment was down in six months' time, leaving Dr. Val and her faculty to reflect on their mission. Dr. Val asked for a private meeting with Dr. Marty.

"I am concerned about the numbers, Dr. Marty. Since I have been here, we have been a school that served the disenfranchised. We have a solid name for developmental education at AACC, and our students come here looking for that support. Our enrollment is down; our faculty are leaving. We are getting a reputation across St. Louis."

Dr. Marty swiveled around in his chair. "Well, I am glad you have made yourself known. I wasn't sure if you were on board or not, and now I see."

Dr. Val retorted, "I am on the side of our students."

"Wrong answer," Dr. Marty said. You need to be on the side of your President. You know it is customary for the President to ask for the resignation of all Vice Presidents, and then ask them to come back on. I didn't do that. I have watched to see who would fall in line and who would fall aside, and I have watched you fall aside." My philosophy is that we provide a strong academic program, regardless of ethnicity or student preparation. If they are ready for our strong academic program, they stay. When the word gets around, they won't bother to apply. Faculty and staff who can embrace this new paradigm, the new GCC culture, will stay and those who can't …"

Dr. Val suddenly realized that her career hung in the balance. What she thought would be a collegial yet direct conversation on student enrollment trends, had turned into a not-so-veiled threat to her position as Vice President.

Dr. Marty continued, "I understand that you have tenure, so of course you can return to the Math Department. You are welcomed to take leave for the rest of the term and return for the Winter quarter."

Dr. Val could not be more surprised. She had heard other Vice Presidents talk of Dr. Marty's abrupt nature, but none of them lost their position because of it. She found it no coincidence, that she was let go as the only black on the cabinet.

Val took the last six weeks of the fall term to recoup from her fall from grace. She was in touch with the math chair to regain her full course load, mostly at night since her faculty assignments were already set. She didn't want to force others with less time into less-desirable time slots. She knew that Vice Presidents could be let go, but she was the only one.

* * * * *

Val had originally taken her removal from the executive office as a common causality in upper level administration. Vice Presidents come and go all the time. She had never had six weeks off to relax — ever — even in high school. She chalked this up to a chance to return her students and her department. During her time off over the holidays, she spent more time with her mother and Raul. She had a chance to visit her father's grave. She even took in an uncustomary trip to a spa in New Mexico. In many ways, Val originally saw this as a blessing, a righting of the universe to reinstall her back with the community, with the people.

When Val returned to campus in January, she eased into her routine. She set up her faculty office and got into the groove of faculty meetings. She met with several union representatives to get re-acclimated. "Nice to have you back Val, we need you. Perhaps you will see this fight from the underbelly. Do the math." She found this comment to be curious, but took note. Over the next month, she saw other African-Americans leaving abruptly. The Director of Enrollment, gone with three days notice. The Dean of Alumni Affairs, gone. The Associate Dean of Vocational Services left without saying goodbye. These people may not have been bosom buddies, but they were important colleagues of the GCC community. The words echoed in Val's head, "do the math."

Val knew the Associate Director of HR and called in a favor. Stating that she needed the information for accreditation purposes, she asked to see all demographic information on the staff who had been separated from GCC in the last two years, and the dates of their separation. She also requested a staff census; this would allow her to see the last seven months since Dr. Marty had been on board, and over a full year of employment trends before he came aboard. All Val could think of was the message from her union buddy, "do the math."

After studying the numbers for a week, Val saw a statistically significant change in the demographics of GCC after Dr. Marty had come on board. Right before Dr. White passed, the GCC staff of 706 included 121 blacks, or 17%. Within six months of Dr. White's death, the number fluctuated. Three resigned, but two more blacks were hired. When Dr. Marty came aboard, the 699-member GCC staff included 120 blacks, still roughly 17%. However, over the next seven months, all blacks at the Dean's level or higher were eliminated, either by separation or demotion. Sixteen Associate Deans, Deans, Assistant Vice Presidents and Vice Presidents, including Val, were affected. What Val found more compelling was that the number of African-Americans declined from 120 to 71, representing a drop from 17% to just over 10%. Dr. Marty and his tactics had brought systemic racism to the campus, a campus which once served students of color, the disenfranchised, those who needed to see other people of color succeed so they knew they could succeed themselves. Val knew in her gut that the culture of GCC was changing for the worse, and these numbers confirmed her suspicions.

Without prejudice or emotion, Dr. Valencia Jones took her data and the details of her own personal demotion to the Missouri Commission on Human Rights (MCHR), which would lead to a joint filing with the EEOC. GCC was a school that relied on federal dollars in grants and student loans to keep its doors open. The idea of being tagged with racial discrimination in a city like St. Louis would force the Board of Trustees into action. Val's motivation wasn't even about her own well-being. She had tenure, and was able to retake her place in the union. Since she was relieved of administrative duties, she had more time to start her consulting firm. Her concern was for those who could not defend themselves.

The initial meeting with MCHR took less than an hour. She detailed how she was harassed, while the white members of the cabinet were not. Dr. Val had more degrees and experience than the other Vice Presidents, but was the only Vice President demoted, though she also had the longest-standing service, and served the college regionally and nationally. She had served as interim President during a difficult period after a President's death. Her performance was exemplary. Val also showed the systemic racism where almost half the African-Americans had left GCC in a seven month period.

Dr. Val's intake with MCHR was short, as she had prepared all her papers in advance. MCHR had its intake forms online. She needed to describe the initial complaint, write a detailed summary, and categorize the complaint as race, sex, age or retaliatory. The initial forms asked for a detailed witness list of who should be contacted, and what they might contribute to the case. Before arriving at MCHR, Dr. Val organized her findings to support systemic racism. Her file was substantial and thorough. Once her intake was completed, the MCHR had her sign the complaint and gave her an MCHR case number and EEOC case number. They gave her a copy of the signed complaint for her records, and told her the college would be contacted within thirty days.

Returning to campus, Val didn't wait the 30 days for the college to be notified by MCHR; she personally sent a copy of her complaint to Dr. Marty and directly to the board of trustees. She knew the board president personally and added a handwritten note: "While I never wish to bring shame to GCC, the voice of the MCHR is the only one you will hear at this point."

Word washed over campus for the next few days. Everyone knew she had filed a complaint with an outside party. Some faculty avoided Val at all cost; others gave her a knowing handshake and nod, thanking her for her actions. Her union members took up the matter, stating this complaint was one of several reasons to call for a vote of no confidence for Dr. Marty.

The campus was at a standstill, almost polarized by the complaint. The environment did not become warmer for people of color, as faculty and staff of color continued to leave campus. Dr. Marty and his abrupt manner still made people uncomfortable, though he had endured several grueling meetings with the board to stop the exodus of color at GCC. When people are uncomfortable, they become defensive and anxious. The campus climate had changed from a welcoming and inclusive one, to one where people worked with doors closed and caller ID in place. Everyone was scared.

The students noticed the difference as well, and developed their own enclave in the cafeteria or student offices. The delicate balance of faculty, students and staff had been fractured, as everyone was poised to watch their back.

MCHR continued to request office documents from GCC. Their efforts to corroborate Dr. Val's notes and findings were exhaustive for the HR staff at GCC. They were copying notes, holding meetings, and disclosing statistics typically reserved for the ten year accreditation visit.

After nine months, MCHR attempted to schedule the first conciliation meeting. Dr. Marty was instructed by the board to keep quiet and not attend; meanwhile the faculty discovered the dates and circulated a memo of support for the faculty and students of color.

We are saddened by the recent shift in our culture which is culminating in an external review of our campus by the Missouri Commission on Human Rights. With heavy hearts, we are hoping for closure to this rift so we as faculty and staff, as a community, might heal. We have always been a campus that included all races, colors and creeds. We need to defend our ideals against all threats, internal and external. We ask that all in our community move to reconcile, and reconnect.

The fervor across campus was a critical factor in the administration's refuting the meeting. Nonetheless, the numbers did not lie. GCC had engaged in systemic racism. Despite their efforts to recruit and retain staff and faculty of color, the next six months proved to repeat the same patterns. GCC was becoming more and more vanilla by the day. Dr. Val continued to work at the reduced salary of faculty. She was making easily 55% less than she made as a Vice President.

MCHR and EEOC generated a Right to Sue Letter 13 months after the filing. It was clear that the investigation was not over and that the administration was stubborn, despite the statistical evidence. Dr. Val had anticipated as much and had started investigating employment attorneys. She was prepared to fight to the end.

About two months after the Right to Sue Letter was issued, Dr. Val found an attorney, Garrick Parks, who agreed to take the case. Together they prepared a demand letter to send to Dr. Marty and the board.

Fr: *Arch Legal Associates, Garrick Parks, Lead Counsel*

Re: *Dr. Valencia Jones, charges of discrimination at GCC*

Case: EEOC No. 19S200750991

MCHR Case No. 20060080867

Dr. Valencia Jones offers this written demand in the matter of Jones v, GCC. GCC has engaged in systematic racism and has discriminated against Dr. Jones, demoted her unlawfully solely because of her race in violation of Federal and Missouri State anti-discrimination laws.

The facts of the case are:

- *Dr. Valencia Jones is a long-standing member of the GCC community. Through the years she has served well as faculty, department chair and vice president. She also served the campus well as interim president.*
- *July 1, 2005, Dr. Martin Hayes was installed as the 7th president of Gateway Community College.*
- *Dr. Hayes engaged in continuous and pervasive harassment of Dr. Jones.*
- *No other cabinet member endured the same treatment*
- *November 15, 2005, Dr. Jones was terminated from her position as Vice President for Academic Affairs and returned to faculty at 55% reduction in salary.*

Facts regarding systemic racism

- *There were 121 blacks on staff of 706 GCC staff, 17 % in 2004, prior to Dr. Hayes' installation*
- *In the seven months subsequent to Hayes' appointment, all blacks*

at the Dean's level or higher were eliminated, by separation or demotion

- *Sixteen (16) Associate Dean, Deans, Assistant Vice President and Vice Presidents, including Dr. Jones, were affected.*
- *Overall, the number of African-Americans declined from 120 to 71, meaning the number declined from 17% to just over 10%.*

Dr. Jones has retained an attorney and a "right to sue letter" from MCHR on this matter.

Dr. Jones is aware of the authority in the MCHR to order payment of back pay, from the date of termination to the date of settlement. To date that amount is $93,000, and the corresponding GCC contribution to her TIAA-CREF.

Dr. Jones is concerned about the welfare of the community of color, requesting a full diversity assessment five year plan to help restore the college's inclusive culture.

Dr. Jones has served as a loyal member of the GCC community for over 20 years. She is disheartened that she has been left no choice but to engage in these proceedings. While she is saddened, her commitment to GCC does not lessen her resolve to seek proper resolution.

Dr. Jones awaits the response from GCC through her attorney Garrick Parks, of Arch Legal Associates of St. Louis, MO. We are prepared to engage in further legal action. Attached please see our preparation to file in district court.

Within two weeks of receiving the letter, GCC legal counsel caved in. They called Mr. Parks to engage in settlement agreements. Dr. Val felt as though they had finally turned a corner. It seemed that GCC simply did not want a lawsuit filed. The whole community had watched their campus decrease in diversity over the last three years. Dr. Val was a very public figure who had the long-standing respect of the community. She was a home town favorite with grass roots support. A lawsuit and endless dispositions was not a favorable situation for the campus. They responded with the following:

To: Arch Legal Associates, Garrick Parks, Lead Counsel

Re: Dr. Valencia Jones, charges of discrimination at GCC

Case: EEOC No. 19S200750991

MCHR Case No. 20060080867

RELEASE FROM LIABILITY AND AGREEMENT FOR SETTLEMENT

THIS RELEASE FROM LIABILITY AND AGREEMENT FOR SETTLEMENT is developed and will be executed between Dr. Valencia Jones and Gateway Community College; respectively "Dr. Jones" and "GCC" Collectively, GCC and Dr. Jones will be referred to in this **RELEASE FROM LIABILITY AND AGREEMENT FOR SETTLEMENT** as the "Parties."

 Points of the case:
> Dr. Jones is currently employed by GCC;

> Dr. Jones alleged that GCC has engaged in systemic racism over the last three years;

> GCC denies any wrongdoing or illegal conduct with respect to Dr. Jones or its employment practices in total;

> The Missouri Commission on Human Rights investigated Dr. Jones' allegations (MCHR Case No. 20060080867) and GCC's responses;

> Federal Equal Employment Opportunity Commission also had before it a joint-filed Charge of Discrimination (EEOC No. 19S200750991) alleging the same types of claims;

> Both Parties are currently represented by counsel;

> Through a series of meetings, both parties have come to a mutual agreement.

> **BELOW PLEASE FIND RELEASE FROM LIABILITY AND AGREEMENT FOR SETTLEMENT** which will set the terms. These items are legally binding. Both parties understand that they will be subject to litigation or possible termination of this agreement if the terms set forth are breeched. With this stipulation in mind, the parties will agree to the following:

GCC has no admission or finding of liability

The entering into this **RELEASE FROM LIABILITY AND AGREEMENT FOR SETTLEMENT** prior to trial or arbitration is an effort only to conclude this matter without further cost or delay. GCC has no admission of any wrongdoing or any other improper activity. The entering into this **RELEASE FROM LIABILITY AND AGREEMENT FOR SETTLEMENT** shall not be construed as an admission of liability or wrongdoing by either Party. Nothing contained in this **RELEASE FROM LIABILITY AND AGREEMENT FOR SETTLEMENT** shall be deemed to establish or identify a "Prevailing Party."

Conclusion of the Action

Dr. Jones, through her counsel, shall file all necessary papers with the MCHR and the Equal Employment Opportunity Commission to discontinue with prejudice and as settled all her disputes with GCC. This formal withdrawal should occur within three weeks after GCC has disbursed the payments discussed in the **RELEASE FROM LIABILITY AND AGREEMENT FOR SETTLEMENT**

GCC will pay $45,000 plus restore the match $15000 to Dr. Jones' TIAA-CREF retirement account. The $15,000 is not subject to taxation, as any contribution to retirement. Dr. Jones' $45,000 will be disbursed on a 1099. The attorney's fees of $27,000 will also be distributed to Garrick Parks on a 1099.

Privacy & Confidentiality

As Dr. Jones will remain a full-time staff member at GCC, it is critical that both parties will not disparage each other or discuss any terms of this release and settlement.

Finality of agreement

RELEASE FROM LIABILITY AND AGREEMENT FOR SETTLEMENT offers the entire series of elements and factors between the Parties with respect to the settlement of all matters between them. Any and all previous discussions, agreements, negotiation, written or oral are neutralized by this release. This release from liability agreement may only be revised in writing and must be agreed upon by all parties. Such acceptance and agreement are only designated by written and notarized signature.

Once both parties have reviewed, signed and notarized six original copies, the dispute between both parties will legally be considered resolved.

Let it be settled hence forth....

* * * * *

In addition to monetary damages, GCC committed to corrective measures which included the development of a diversity committee, with faculty, students and staff. Diversity initiatives were infused into the curriculum. All divisions had to subscribe to diversity training. HR underwent an audit to review hiring policies. Val thought it was amazing; none of these corrective measures were needed under Dr. White, who simply fostered a sense of inclusion on every level. But with a new close-minded president, all these changes were forced on a campus that would resent being required to act as human beings. The campus itself was a victim. A campus climate is a mirror image of the president's philosophy. Search committees for faculty and administrative staff had selected their candidates to support the president's agenda that had generated a diversity deprived campus climate.

Val won her part of the settlement in back pay. She donated half of it to her beloved developmental math center. Dr. Marty stayed on for six months after the settlement. Under his leadership, the campus was never the same. Staff remained guarded and standoffish. The union made a point to play hard ball during contract negotiations, as it did not trust the good will of administration.

Once Dr. Marty resigned, GCC conducted a national presidential search choose a Latina woman as its 8th president. Only after Dr. Marty's departure could the campus begin healing and return to an inclusive environment. It would take time; do the math.

Chapter 8

Daphne Kimiko—Documenting wire fences in the museum

In tough economic times, often employers are looking for ways to demote or even separate employees. While it is an employer's right to do so, if the employer proceeds with disparate treatment or without proper documentation, the employee can have cause for legal complaint.

In converse, employees' records are critical as well. Keep notes from meetings. Keep performance evaluations or any other written records discussing performance. Keep a copy of the organization's discrimination policy, anti-retaliation policy (if one exists) and progressive discipline policies. An employee has a right to keep records on notes pertaining to them personally. Were there five men in the department, but only the one woman was let go? Did everyone else receive a written performance appraisal, but the only Jewish employee received no such evaluation before facing termination? Are other people in the same protected class leaving the organization? For example, did 35% of the women resign from the same department; perhaps a large number of Hispanics requested transfers to another area? These statistics can help an employee make a case for systematic racism or sexism.

It is unlikely that any employee is fortunate enough to spend his or her entire working career without an employment issue. Everyone will eventually be in a protected class, either by race, sex, religion or other background, or they simply grow into a protected class once reaching 40 years of age. Proper documentation and timelines can

*help an employee make a sound case, and show the strength of such
a case if such notes are needed to work with a Human Relations
Commission or an attorney.*

As if the Japanese didn't face discrimination in the first place, the bombing of
Pearl Harbor, December 7, 1941 brought a rush of hate for all Asian people,
Japanese, Chinese and Korean. Discrimination was riding like a tsunami
through their typically uneventful everyday lives. In addition to the jeers in
the street and an occasional rock thrown in their direction, after the bombing
the Japanese endured the formal racial insults which riddled the papers in
racialized political cartoons. The Japanese were called yellow 'snakes,'
'devils,' and 'bandits.' Despite the fact that many Japanese had never been to
Japan and had their families and loyalties on American soil, they were treated
like a pestilence in their own neighborhoods. The resulting paranoia from
the United States Government led them to sequester over 110,000 Japanese-
Americans, ripping them from their homes, relocating them to remote and
bleak housing in the desolate windswept lands of the American interior.
After Pearl Harbor, the government hurriedly built close to 20 internment
and isolation camps in the desolate areas of states like New Mexico, Texas,
Montana, and Wyoming for those with even 1/16th of their lineage traced to a
Japanese blood line.

With only days' notice, families were notified of their forced relocation.
Small children watched their friends taken to other camps. College students
were forced to withdraw only months from earning a degree. Families lost all
personal belongings: clothes, radios, refrigerators, and furniture. All worldly
possessions were sacrificed on short notice.

The conditions at the internment camps were horrid, with only one light
bulb hanging from inside each of the barracks and paper thin walls stuffed
with cardboard for insulation. The government was in such a rush to extract
the Japanese, the housing was poorly built, and made for a pitiful shelter
from the whipping winds of the cold desert winters. Many families endured
such conditions for four years. While the government issued typhoid shots to
prevent disease, the same care was not taken with food. The Japanese stood

in the cold to eat horrible food from tin pie plates. They ate the Army surplus of ketchup, hot dogs, Spam and potatoes. Those over the age of twelve were not even given milk. Such rations gave rise to Japanese modifications to Spam sushi and weenie royale. As the Japanese diet was wiped out, these make shift dishes were an attempt to retain some sense of culture. Diarrhea was a common occurrence. Many of the Japanese spent extensive time combating loose bowels in these conditions. Daphne's parents met as youngsters in this squalor. Playing as children in the gang mess hall, they adjusted and persevered. When the government finally released the Japanese and offered make shift apologies, Daphne's parents still remained close, and Rose and her mother moved back to San Francisco as did Tommy's parents.

Daphne's art was influenced by this melancholy that she rightfully inherited from her parents. She was an artistically gifted child who grew up in the 1970s, in San Francisco. Daphne's mother, Rose Suzuki who was only half Japanese and half white, married Tommy Kimiko in the mid-1960s. Sit-ins, protests, and riots marked the early days of Kim's Grocery. As their own family was still rebuilding from the total disruption of the 1940s, America was enduring national unrest through the 1950s and 1960s. In the midst of such turmoil, the Kimikos built a life together in the Jtown section of San Francisco. Unlike the neighborhood before the war, Jtown was a mix of Japanese, blacks and other migrants who came to the empty neighborhood when the Japanese were forced into internment camps. Tommy Kimiko came back to the neighborhood to reestablish his grocery in a growing San Francisco which seemed to be a magnet for difference and change. Not only was the civil rights movement in full swing, but the gay rights movement and ERA were also played out in the streets of San Francisco. Rose Kimiko wanted to maintain a quiet life; she was the product of an interracial marriage and had endured a great deal of bias from all communities. However, Tommy was a forward thinker and could see the application of social protest, whether gay, Black, Asian, or Native American. Marginalized populations were always fighting for their rights in the United States. He reminded his family of the time when the Japanese faced persecution just for being different.

Through her early years, Daphne painted, winning various art contests and shows in museums by 16. She was a bit of an artistic genius. She won pop art competitions such as "Heart in San Francisco," and "Save the Petrified Forest." She placed highly in California statewide contests and received honorable mention in a California/Japan joint sponsored competition and gallery exhibit. She dabbled with wood block designs, and also had some success with origami. Her use of color and lines had an old Asian slant, with a modern touch that caught the eye of several art enthusiasts in the region. Her aesthetic was a Katsushika Hokusai meets early O'Keefe.

Tommy Kimiko still insisted that his daughter earn a Bachelor's degree, to enhance her natural talent in the arts. Instead of sending her to the Art Institute of San Francisco, he sent his daughter to the University of California, Berkeley. She won partial scholarship for pastels and oil painting. Her style reflected her artistic flare, colors and jewel tones. Daphne had grown into a voluptuous woman, curvy with hips, standing a statuesque 5'8." Her mom said she got that American body given all the junk food Daphne ate as a kid and the Caucasian blood from her grandfather. But Daphne's father reminded her that her artistic talent came honestly from his own father's poetry and calligraphy.

Daphne graduated with a double major in fine arts and classics. In addition to her solid academic work, Daphne volunteered in the university's museum. She learned the inner workings of museum operations in addition to procedures for art acquisition. With her father's urging, she interned at a number of museums and art galleries during the summers. These experiences helped her in understanding gallery maintenance and working with client gifts and events. Upon graduation, she had established a career with experiences that equaled close to three years' professional experience. With her focus, she was able to land a job as an assistant curator at a museum in suburban San Francisco.

During her time at Cobalt Light Gallery, she worked well with clients. The gallery owner, Devon Crafter, was a bit of a hippie. She saw Crafter's old pictures from Woodstock, smoking weed in his VW bug. He was formerly a walking cliché for free love and nonconformity. She admired his "out of the box" thinking, and his ability to make connections across the country.

She didn't like the way he would occasionally fall back into his old ways and tweak her behind or pet her hair. She didn't believe in all that free love; typically, she tried to ignore him to get along. She received an occasional email asking for drinks. Daphne was offended, and simply responded "Sorry, I have plans with family," and deleted email flirtations. One day she was so frustrated and commented to him directly, "Doesn't your wife mind? I mean, you are married."

Devon Crafter responded, "She understands, in fact we are swingers. She asked me if you would want to come over sometime." Crafter followed up with a handwritten post it on her computer, asking her to meet up with him and his wife for Sunday brunch. Daphne narrowed her eyes in disgust, huffed to herself and crumbled the note for the trash.

Daphne loved the art museum and the clients, but was put off by and blushed at the continuous sexual suggestions. She was not from a prudish culture, but she also knew not to fish off the company pier. There was not enough pot in the world for her to "swing" with her boss and his wife. First, she didn't swing AC/DC, and second, she just wasn't sharing herself like that.

Daphne developed various artist openings over the next 18 months. At each gallery opening, Devon Crafter approached her again with a proposition of swinging. In fact, he brought his wife, Sally, to check out the scene. Sally looked like an updated version of her younger self. The sun had weathered her skin to leather-like appearance, though it still kept a healthy tan. Sally obviously had had a breast augmentation, and wore clingy clothes more appropriate for someone 15 years her junior.

"Hi Daphne," Sally said, "My... hmm...Devon didn't do you justice — you are beautiful."

Daphne realized she was being hit on, and tried to dart away to take care of some of the clients entering the gallery..."Ah, well, thanks, but I gotta..."

"I don't mean to offend you, but I saw Memoirs of a Geisha. I have to say, you women are just beautiful. I don't mean to offend you, Daphne, I just, I had to see you and hope you can join us after the opening."

Daphne realized Sally was high as a kite on weed and propositioning her at work. She didn't want to shoot her down, but this was not her style. Free love or not, the 60s were over. And Devon Crafter needed to leash his wife. Daphne nodded and slipped away. She made a point to keep herself on the other side of the gallery throughout the evening. She was relieved when Sally and Devon Crafter left, as he often exited to let Daphne close a few deals and then close the gallery. She had dodged the bullet again, but realized that she needed to find another museum. She didn't want to make waves or complain, but she didn't want sex with Devon Crafter and his swinging wife. She thought about writing a note, but this small museum didn't have a human resources person. What? What was she going to complain to the boss about the boss? She was trapped.

Daphne's work remained exemplary. Devon Crafter commented on such and said he could even forego formal evaluations. 'Everything was fine, no worries' he would always say. She had made connections with the artist community through the state and took the museum from a simple neighborhood space to a museum that received state wide attention and even national respect.

During the intensity of promoting the museum, Daphne stopped her job search and focused on enhancing her profile through the museum. She was working longer hours and expanding her network.

That summer, the owner, Mr. Devon Crafter hired his son part-time. Jake was a walking hard on, and just didn't have the restraint his father had. Devon and Sally had at least stopped asking Daphne — ok after four or five advances, but they had stopped. Though Jake was seven years her junior, he persisted in asking Daphne out for lunch, for dinner, for a snack, a trip to the vending machine, to the convenience store down the street. Jake's pursuit was intense, but Daphne said nothing. This was a different game. Instead of pushing back a mature man and his horny wife, she had to keep her guard up at work constantly with a very forward 21-year old. Her sole relief was that he only reported to work three days of the six days that Daphne worked. Daphne did everything she could to be understated on the days Jake reported in. At home, she had begun writing up the information on Jake's advances, but her heart wasn't in it. She searched for jobs, cruised the Bloomingdale's website, and often fell asleep exhausted. She planned time out of the office with clients, stayed in the open space, just trying to get through the summer waiting for Jake to return to school and stop working for his dad.

One day Jake was in the office complaining about how he didn't understand a database. He was frustrated and pacing in his small office. Devon Crafter walked by and offered a quick solution, "Daphne knows this database inside and out. Have her come in here."

Daphne couldn't escape. She had to follow the boss's order. She came in the office to see the devilish smile on Jake's face, almost like a check mate. Devon Crafter commented, "There, problem solved. Daphne, I know you can coach my son." Devon left.

They started slowly with Daphne standing on the far side of the room, trying to coach Jake through logging in, entering the key code, and inputting data. He continued with his frustrated antics. "How am I supposed to learn this? Maybe I should have Dad send me to training."

Daphne heard the veiled threat. There was no way Devon Crafter wanted to pay to send his son for training on a program that Daphne knew so well. She crossed the room, and began trying to walk him through the database functions. Jake still squirmed and protested. He didn't understand key codes, he couldn't figure out queries. He couldn't do anything right. In her own frustration, Daphne leaned over his shoulder and took the mouse, showing him a few critical functions. Despite wearing a minimizing bra, her breast rubbed against his shoulder. She was so embarrassed. He was obviously aroused and turned to her. "See I knew you liked me! Quit frontin'!"

Daphne was trapped. She backed off, "Stop it, I told you! What is it with your family!" They were both stunned. They both knew she was talking about the oversexed nature of the entire family. She regained her composure, and then she continued with the instructions from across the room.

Jake was embarrassed too, that his affection and advances were unwelcomed, again. He was an insecure 21-year old who had little luck with girls. He had been rejected time and time again in high school and at trade school. He took up body building as a way to compensate, but it did not make up for his personality. He just knew that he could bag this Asian babe, smart, pretty; but she wouldn't even look at him, wouldn't even grab coffee, and now she had the nerve to tease him, knowing she would never return the favor. Daphne quickly ended the database lesson and left the museum for an extended lunch.

Jake reported Daphne to his father, claiming sexual harassment, claiming that she flirted with him. His feelings were crushed and he used every ounce of frustration to paint a colorful story of how some buxom Japanese art-eest led him on. Jake also told the slam Daphne had said about the family, that they were "oversexed." He went so far as to say that she was asking him to dinner, she was asking him to lunch, and that he was turning her down. She was giving him difficult assignments, things that needed extra explanation, extra attention.

A week passed after the awkward incident. Daphne had visited a few vendors across town that week, and had just come in from Sacramento after meeting with a few artists. She had hoped that the whole thing would be forgotten. Despite four years of hard work, Devon Crafter called her in and simply stated that her behavior would not be tolerated. He outlined a series of issues and hearsay that were obviously twisted. He accused her of flirting with staff and wearing revealing clothing. He was happy with her performance, but the sexual prowess she had exhibited was creating a hostile workplace for his staff. He even referenced a comment his wife Sally had made over a year ago when they hit on her and asked her to a swinger's party. Somehow, instead of her being cast as the harassed, she was painted as the aggressor. He had gathered comments from others on the job, who thought her dress and comments were inappropriate.

Daphne was without words. She sat there and let Devon unfurl lie after untruth after lie about her demeanor and character. She thought, 'of course they sided with Jake; he was the boss's son.' She had no recourse. It was an at-will state. But wait, she was the one who was sexually harassed.

Devon Crafter said he would give her a reference and two weeks' pay because she had been a good employee until now. But he could not allow her to continue at the museum. It was too risky; he didn't want a lawsuit from one of the employees. He claimed he was afraid the others would resign if he kept her on staff.

What?! Daphne was the one who was harassed. She didn't even protest. How could she fight the boss's son? She had a reference and two weeks' pay.

Daphne was furious; but had done nothing to protect herself. She knew she should have done something, written something, and documented something. She left the gallery that morning and went to her dad's grocery. When she arrived, her dad was in the back reviewing the books.

"Hi Daddy," Daphne said. She kissed her father as he looked over his half moon glasses.

"Surprised to see you here, Birdie — thought you had a big gallery opening next week. You look nice though."

Daphne had a flash in her eye, focused, and angry. Tommy Kimiko had seen this flash. It was like the look his mother had. Daphne continued, "I was let go today. I am …"

Tommy continued with his daughter, "I know the Crafters were nice, but I told you, you were too trusting."

Daphne sighed, still angry, "His son had been hitting on me all summer, and well, and he finally cornered me, and then reported me as the harasser." Daphne didn't dare tell her father how Sally and Devon Crafter were swingers who had pursued her for two years.

"Hmm, you have a good record with them. I know they have the profile across the city because of you. Did you report it? What did you do here?"

Daphne knew he was right."Report it to where? We don't have that kind of HR support. Daddy, I was already looking for a job. I was focused on leaving. They gave me two weeks' pay and references."

Tommy went through his rolodex and handed his daughter a phone number, "Here, call Mr. Yamura. He and I went to night school together. He is an attorney who works with family law and employment. Give him a call. He'll know you're my daughter."

"How did you know?

Tommy answered, "A father knows when a daughter is in trouble. You left several drafts of your resume at the house last month…"

Daphne left her dad. He was so smart. She should have talked to him before. She called Mr. Yamura who agreed to see her that afternoon. "Bring all your documentation he said." Daphne felt a twang of guilt in her gut.

Mr. Yamura had been an attorney for ten years. He didn't have a flashy practice, but he was well respected in the Japanese community. He greeted Daphne and offered to chat over miso soup and green tea at the café on the street. It was a nice day; he wanted her to feel relaxed.

Daphne repeated her story. She commented on the harassment, the tweaks on the behind, and her performance. Daphne spoke so fast, almost as if speaking fast would minimize the hurt in retelling her story. She went on to talk about being approached for swinging parties the boss held, and talked about his son, Jake.

Mr. Yamura commented, "Do you have a timeline? A copy of your complaint? Something?"

Daphne replied, "We are such a small group. There were not even 30 people working at the museum."

"If there are over 15 people, he is bound by federal law."

"I figured I would just get another job. Just leave."

"But that didn't happen fast enough," Yamura continued. "Your problem, you were too nice. You needed to document, keep records, notes, emails. You needed to complain to someone about how you were the one subjected to a hostile environment."

"But I didn't want to get fired."

Yamara continued, "Yet here we are today, with you fired and no recourse."

Daphne saw the point. She regretted deleting all those flirty emails Devon had sent.

"Well Daphne, at least you got a reference and a good reputation in the artistic community. You even have two weeks' pay. But I also guess that the other employees will not make statements against Jake either."

Daphne was angry, silent, but listening to Yamara.

"The best thing is that you are still young, with references. But I have to tell you, you don't have documentation, I couldn't begin to put a case together on this."

Daphne protested slightly, "But they…"

"Daphne, it's not the truth, it is what truth you can prove. Now you are telling me you have your word against that of several employees of the museum. And you don't have memos, documentation etc., you don't even have copies of your performance evaluations or testimony from clients for your work. You're telling me you didn't even keep a diary of your daily work and what happened. Are there statistics that confirm your stellar performance? Documented raises? He has a right to hire and fire unless there is discrimination. You can't prove discrimination."

"I hate to be defeated before I even start."

Yamara continued, "You are talented, I have seen your work, even bought one of your paintings from your dad. My folks endured that government internment. I know injustice and know how to fight, but we don't have the tools here. My recommendation is to take your reference, your four years' service, and carry these lessons into the next job. I don't give up easily, but there is nothing to get started on."

Daphne left her meeting with Mr. Yamura. She was furious, but knew he would not steer her wrong. Her regrouping included applying for a teaching position with the community college, and looking for a museum position. She helped around the shop, let her apartment go, and moved into her parents' house for a year. She even helped around the grocery on weekends. She was young, and ticked off, but she had learned the hard way to document everything... everything. She would never let this one happen again.

Daphne took her time and landed a curator position at a midsized museum. Mr. Crafter did give her that reference. The museum was impressed with Daphne's talent and education. Daphne also interviewed them. She reviewed their public image and various news articles about them. Daphne also called former clients to inform them she was simply moving on, and also asked of their experiences with this new museum.

Daphne was pleased on her first day. The museum staff bought her flowers and a coffee cake. They could have a little fun; but then they all returned to work. Daphne made a point to consider her staff and key an eye on the staff culture. Nonetheless, before the day ended, she sought out the small Human Resources Department, stopping by just to get acquainted.

Chapter 9

Kansas Ogilvie—Ageism in New England

ADEA, The Age Discrimination in Employment Act of 1967, governs age discrimination, protecting those employees over 40 years of age. The goal is to encourage employers to promote workers based on their ability not their age. The spirit is to prevent ageism, and the problems that emerge for employers with an aging employee base. Several states prohibit age discrimination and may have more stringent laws than the ADEA.

There was no waving wheat off the orange line in Roxbury, Massachusetts, but Kansas Ogilvie grew like a wild weed in Boston's not-so-privileged neighborhood. She was a long time resident, transplanted from the Midwest as a kid. A product of the horrible busing days in greater Boston, her memories of grade school were stained with smashed eggs and rotten tomatoes punched through algebra and world history.

Kansas was a bit taller than average. Her dark brown eyes pierced through her glasses, assessing any situation. Her hair changed like the wind — braids, twists, a baby fro, whatever to keep her neat and crisp in the extremes of Boston's winter. Despite the whipping winds flown on the wings of the winter weather hawk, Kansas had richness to her skin.... If mahogany could be ebony, her rich chocolate complexion was the epitome of perfection. A hard working woman, Kansas worked several odd jobs after high school. She stayed with her parents for a while before venturing out on her own. She had learned the city and its proper place for blacks.

The mosaic of the metro line was almost the color code of safe havens, if you knew how to read it. Orange Line was cool all the way through, just keep only one eye open. Green Line, the education line, traveled to the degrees, money, Chestnut Hill, Newton, ambling past Boston University or Northeastern. Red Line, the border, ran all the way from the Northern "Haw -vad Yaaad" through center city, then south to the shore. The Blue Line can lead to black and blue; don't ever get caught in Southie after dark.

In her late 20s, Kansas married a West Indian immigrant. They met at Mattapan's West Indian festival one year, at the Boston Carnival. With Blue Hill Avenue jammed with dancing, feathered women on parade, steel drums, reggae, and her favorite curried delicacies, Kansas had found a good man. She and Wilford had a fast courtship of maybe seven months before marrying and moving to Brighton. It was a bit outside the city, but close to public transportation, groceries and dry cleaners. He held down two and a half jobs, supporting Kansas and their two boys. He was a good provider. As the boys grew, Kansas picked up her pharmacy technology certificate and started to ease the financial stress in the house. The boys also got odd jobs, making the expensive financial climate in Boston a bit warmer.

Her career flourished over the next ten years. She went to night school and started teaching pharmacy technology at a local family-owned career and technical school. She was well-respected at school and gained quite a reputation for being a solid educator and role model, especially for students of color trying to make a way out of no way and the no where they came from.

Kansas had hit her pinnacle, and was named chair of her department at 47. The school director Casey Mews, threw the party. All 27 faculty attended, even the night instructors. Wilford and the boys, almost grown now, came to see Mom get her promotion, with an excellent service record and a raise to $39,000. Kansas was more than pleased and modeled to her children that hard work and dedication pays off.

Kansas was in seventh heaven. She rewrote the curriculum and recruited new teachers. She was making strides in student retention and assisting her students with career placement. She was exceptional at what she did, and felt she had found her calling. It wasn't Harvard or Tufts, but it was a living.

She took great pride when she was out in the city and saw her own graduates working in a pharmacy or reporting to work at one of the major hospitals.

Eight months later, Mews called a meeting of all the department chairs. The family owners had sold the school to a large corporation. Mews assured them that all jobs would be safe. He forecasted an exciting time ahead, with renovated labs and classrooms. They would all get new computers and a building much closer to public transportation. They should expect their student census to grow, and with success they should expect raises and promotions. His over enthusiasm concerned his co-workers. An era was ending; corporations often meant empty promises.

With suspended belief, Kansas and her fellow staff held fast, and didn't immediately look for jobs elsewhere. They had heard of this type of thing before. Down in Rhode Island, this same corporation bought a few schools in Providence. At first everything looked bright and shiny, but the students complained, and turnover skyrocketed. The staff knew this all too well, as a few of those teachers moved to Boston and found new jobs to escape the parent corporation.

Choosing between the devil they don't know and the devil who is about to take over their school, many decided to stay on through the transition. The first signs of trouble were the ever present school commercials. Daytime, nighttime, anytime, all the time, their new logo and slogan were flashed across all the R & B radio stations, TVLand, BET, and FX. Next, the curriculum changes rolled through, which allowed less time for tutoring one on one and even less time to teach the whole course with two weeks shaved off of each term.

The next blow came with the new changes in the executive staff. First the Financial Aid Director resigned; then the Director of Admissions quit abruptly. The corporate takeover made folks anxious, especially when Director Casey Mews announced his retirement. "You'll be fine, in good hands. The new corporation has more resources. Anyway it was time for me to retire." Even if the staff wanted to believe Mews, his leaving with only three days' notice, and no opportunity for a retirement party, made the staff even more uneasy.

The new director, Jack Peters, a salt and pepper athletic white male in his 50s, joined the staff. He and the new executive replacements were hard core home office representatives. Dressed in pin-striped suits and corporate lapel pins, they talked of students as "starts" and "drops." Students didn't have names; they were reduced to numbers and cohorts. Faculty were headed into countless presentations on how much revenue each "head" or student made the company, and how teachers were responsible for tracking down students at home, even going to their apartments and sending postcards and emails to make sure they don't drop (and taking their financial aid with them).

The upheaval among faculty was enormous, and desperate. Staff feverishly started looking for jobs in their respective industries. Kansas was tired and now facing an accreditation visit as the new corporation was setting up shop. The new director was relentless, yapping after Kansas as she walked down the hall for class. Peters recited start numbers, accreditation issues, and compliance polices, all as Kansas was trying to compose herself for the lecture in front of 25 students. Kansas took note though; the white department chairs did not have to endure this harassment. No one else was publically scrutinized.

Three weeks of nagging from Peters spiked Kansas' blood pressure. Her doctor put her on blood pressure medication and gave her a script for a mild sedative. Two of her six teachers quit under the pressure, leaving Kansas to teach two classes simultaneously in the morning to make sure all sections were covered. Other departments endured the same kind of loss in the teacher ranks. People were unhappy, yet no one was harassed publicly like Kansas was in front of her colleagues and students.

The straw that broke the camel's back occurred when Mr. Peters burst into Kansas' classroom in the middle of class.

He exclaimed, "Drops are up 7%!" He shook his finger in her face, "Do you know what this means? I have been telling you about this problem for weeks! Are you not listening to the words that come out of my mouth? Incompetence on any level will not be tolerated!" Kansas's eye dilated to the size of saucers. She turned and walked out of the classroom, ears ringing, eyes filling with tears. The rest of the morning was a blur. Of that dreadful hour, she only remembered taking her Tweety Bird scrubs, the pictures of her kids, and her pocketbook. Kansas left the building.

Stunned, she called Wilford. "It's an at-will state. Technically he didn't fire you; you walked out, right? They can do what they want. We talked about you leaving anyway with the corporate takeover."

Kansas was beside herself at her husband's words. Gone were the soft sounds of steel drums from years gone by. The clanging gong of reality was sounding in her ear, unyielding, unmerciful.

She conceded, "You're right."

She received a few calls from colleagues, mourning her loss from the staff. They could not believe Mr. Peters forced her out like that. She had done so much for that department, for the curriculum, and for the students. And Mr. Peters was walking around with his chest poked out, like he had accomplished something.

A couple students showed up in her office at school, crying when they heard the news that she was gone. Kansas had become a real role model to those who did not have reliable parents. She had become the stability for many who were excited about school for a change. Because of Kansas, they even stayed in school and believed the promise of internships and job placement.

One student even called her at home, "crying, We're so sorry Ms. Kansas, are you sure you can't come back? It just isn't school with you gone like this."

After a couple weeks, one of Kansas' friends let her come back afterhours to get the rest of her personal items. Kansas couldn't believe it. Twelve years she gave this place. She took a glimpse at all the pictures of graduating classes, students who had come back with their kids and even their moms and aunts to brag about what a difference this education made. It was all gone. Can't judge a building by its cover; new structures and renovations did not create a safe work environment.

Kansas continued her job hunt, demoralized; she cried a bit only when the boys were out to school or work. Wilford quickly grew tired of coaching her through the loss.

"Quit yo' blood clot cryin'; girl, let it go. They didn't deserve you anyway."

She did receive an occasional update from the school about who resigned and who was fired. Only one of her original teachers remained. A couple teachers went to New York, and one took a maternity leave; it just wasn't the same staff. Maybe Kansas wasn't meant to be there.

About three months later, right before the holidays, she met with a former colleague and girlfriend, Lindsey, to catch up.

Lindsey said, "Giiirrrllll! I ain't neva lied! You should see who Mr. Peters hired to replace you!"

"I'm not interested," Kansas said, still wounded, yet a wave of curiosity swelled in her throat.

"You should see her, some 20 something blonde chick with that new Jennifer Aniston haircut. She can't be 30 yet. And with only two years experience from Boston General! But the catch, check this! They are paying her $59,000."

"What?! That's $20,000 more than they ever paid me, even after 12 years' service."

"Kansas, she doesn't even have teaching duties. They hired four more teachers, she is just an administrator. Less work, more pay. She never taught before."

"Lindsey, how do you know all this?"

"Kansas, you know Carla can't hold hot water. She processed the paperwork. The new chair started last week, big hair and all! Maybe that extra money is for salon products!"

"You mean they hired a white girl with a thimble of experience, and half my age, to pay her $20,000 more?"

"That's the word. They didn't even have black or Hispanic candidates. Think she is the daughter of one of Mr. Peter's friends, not sure."

There was a heat wave in Kansas. She could feel her heart beating through her eyeballs. Her vision blurred, and she was beyond stunned. Aren't there rules against this kind of thing? Sure Boston is a racist place, but dag.

Kansas barely touched her food. Just as Carla couldn't hold hot water, neither could Lindsey. They chatted about simple stuff, what the kids were getting for Easter, the ridiculous winter Nor'easter's in Boston and the strike being threatened by "T" workers. The conversation was like a soundtrack of babble, with Kansas' mind working in the background. Two hours later, after idle chit chat and marginal food, the two parted ways.

As they left the café, Lindsey lifted her head to the sky and put out her hand. "Yep, that's Boston for ya! Snow for Easter." The flakes had just started falling. Kansas nodded the affirmative, "See ya."

Kansas rode the Green Line home, her mind working to figure out the next steps. Once in Brighton, she made a bee-line to her computer to look up the Massachusetts Commission Against Discrimination (MCAD). She read over the website, reviewing the discriminatory charges, race, sex, age. In the Commonwealth of Massachusetts, complainants had 300 days to file; she certainly was within that timeline. Her mind was reeling. Should she really do this? Should she stay in her place and just be quiet? She would pray on it, and not ask Wilford.

Three days passed and it was Easter Sunday. She sat up in church with that same lump in her throat. Ordinarily her mind was on the honey-baked spiral ham waiting at her mother-in-law's. Now, she only thought and prayed for guidance. The sermon closed with a message about how the persecuted would rise again, the stone shall be rolled away, and we will be made whole. That spark entered Kansas' eye.

First thing Monday morning, after seeing her family off, Kansas rode the "T" downtown to file her case. Her intake form told stories of racial harassment. Despite her excellent service record, Mr. Peters drove her into the ground, berating her in front of her class and colleagues. No white staff member endured such treatment and public humiliation. Kansas claimed constructive discharge and age discrimination. Her salient point was the hiring of a less-qualified white woman who was half her age and paid $20,000 more. The intake MCAD officer took her signature and described the procedures. Her former employer had 30 days to respond. Kansas should expect them to deny everything. An investigation would begin. The MCAD officer informed her that such things take a long time, over a year. Maybe her former employer would grow tired and just settle, but don't count on it.

The intake officer asked Kansas what she wanted as a remedy, to make her whole.

She responded, "A year's salary, a year's retirement, a year's health and eligibility to rehire, and a formal apology."

The intake officer asked, "Would you really want to work for these people again?"

Thirty-five days later, she received a copy of her employer's response. They recognized the authority of the MCAD, and acknowledged that Mr. Peters was the new director, and Kansas was the former Chair of the Pharmacy Technology Department. After those statements, nothing else was consistent with Kansas' statements.

Kansas called former colleagues and asked them to serve as witnesses in the investigation. She collected her paystubs and letters of recommendation and praise from Casey Mews, her former director. She even had cards and letters from former students proving her character and commitment to the school. Kansas had the new company's policy on anti-discrimination, and times and dates of when Mr. Peters berated her in class. The environment was so hostile, Kansas was put on medication. She was locked out of meetings and cut out of decisions made by the other chairs, as she mysteriously was not informed of the change in staff meetings.

Kansas wept to herself, reliving this horrid part of her career. She had worked so hard, been so committed to the school and education, for it all to be whittled down to papers, cards, paystubs and complaints. Though she knew this fight was the right thing, it knotted up her stomach.

Six months after her complaint was filed, Kansas learned that the Assistant Director, La'Toya in Financial Aid, had also filed a race discrimination complaint. Kansas did not know La'Toya well, but knew she had some hard times after her own Director of Financial Aid left. Kansas called La'Toya for coffee.

"Did you know you were the first of ten blacks or Hispanics people to leave that place Kansas? Even the Asian chick left."

Kansas was shocked, because her girlfriend Lindsey hadn't offered any of this information seven months ago before Easter. "Well, what is going on there, La'Toya?"

"They got comfortable. Mr. Peters got real bold when he hired that blonde chick. Threw all kinda money at her. And you know, she can't even teach. When her instructors kept resigning, she couldn't fill in. She didn't have certification qualifying her to teach. And sure as hell didn't have the personality. When Mr. Peters asked her about it, she quit on the spot."

"Humph… couldn't hack it."

"And then your complaint hit. It seems right before Memorial Day; hmmm I know we were not supposed to know, but we all knew. Carla told. Mr. Peters had to meet with legal. This when a team of lawyers from the home office swooped in on him. The business office was scrambling getting records, copying, interviewing the chairs. It was like a fire drill; we all knew it was about you."

Kansas was smiling inside; they were gonna` listen now.

"All of a sudden all these memos were coming from home office about commitment to diversity, about how Human Resources is there to help us. No one believes that shit. I had gone to Human Resources twice about Mr. Peters. He asked me out, squeezed my butt, refused to give me a raise even though I processed more packages than anyone else in there… I filed too. My husband marched in there one day and told off Peters. We packed up my stuff and left."

Kansas found herself envious of the support, but lapping up all the details of Peters' demise.

"I hear two weeks later, late on Friday afternoon, legal swooped in there and told Peters to pack up his things. He was gone, like the Colts leaving Baltimore. No one really knew what happened until Monday morning when they found his office open and all his personal things gone."

"La'Toya how do you know all this?"

"You know Carla called me."

"So did the people at work stop talking to you?"

"Kansas, I don't give a damn. Yes, trifling…. My husband and I were talking about starting a family. Seemed to be the time. I was gonna leave, and say nothing. But I know Peters is wrong. He harassed a number of black people in there; I couldn't walk away. And then I found out you were filing a complaint. I figured strength in numbers, teach that damn corporation something."

Kansas was glad for the unexpected compatriot. They finished their coffee, exchanged numbers, and agreed to stay in touch.

* * * * *

Life moved on. It was two and a half years since Kansas was termination and close to two years since she filed her formal complaint. Kansas saw her eldest son graduate from high school. She took a part time job at the hospital teaching new pharmacy technicians. It wasn't the same, but it was something. Her former employer blew off the first conciliation hearing and offered some pittance of a settlement, something like $2000. Her severance pay with 12 years of service should have been five times at much.

Kansas knew this process was messy, and a lesson in patience and endurance. She sought the informal pro bono advice of an attorney that La'Toya referred. With some reflection, they both decided to stand their ground. Another six months passed of missed phone calls from the MCAD, and delayed responses from the employer's attorney. She was angry and wanted to have the thing done and over; yet she was still living in the shadow of a derailed career.

Time passed, and several meetings and letters later, MCAD called her with a final number. They will give you 3/4 year's pay, and six months' medical coverage. Kansas was relieved, yet dumbfounded; this multi-million dollar company was fighting her over $30,000?

The MCAD representative commented, "At least you don't pay an attorney a third of your settlement. I know you had to wait; this is probably the best you will get from them. Talk it over with your family, and let me know in three days."

Kansas had nothing to discuss. She would take the $30,000. It put her in a position to pay for her son's tuition to U Mass Boston. The timing had a silver lining, though her own career was still on life support. She also called La'Toya. While she did admit to the matter being closed, the confidentiality statements forbade her from disclosing details. La'Toya and Kansas weren't that tight anyway. La'Toya was happy. She did receive some money, and apparently enough to outfit her nursery for her baby that was due in a few weeks. Time sure did pass.

Another three months passed in arguments about settlement language, right to hire, and defamation. Kansas was through. It was a tough road and if she had it to do again, she would have started looking for a job sooner. But she still would have filed the complaint to teach Mr. Peters a lesson. People shouldn't be treated this way.

And Kansas wasn't quite the same. She had won her case, but what she lost was gone before she ever filed her complaint. The American dream that her husband came here for was twisted, perverted for the' haves,' and a misnomer for 'have-nots.' She understood why he could not join in this fight with her. It would have unraveled everything; Wilford believed about this country and its ideals about freedom and opportunity.

Her son majored in biology. With Kansas' settlement, he gave up his part-time job and really focused on those books. He made the Dean's List and became a member of Phi Beta Kappa. With his grade point average, he was awarded a scholarship to medical school. That $30,000 didn't make Kansas whole, but it paved the way for opportunity in another way. She smiled at her son's graduation, a doctor in the family. She fought the good fight, and made a way for those coming up after her.

Chapter 10

Adrienne Foxhall—Carolina blues and business necessity

Impulsive or emotional decisions to separate an employee from an organization can cost the employer financially to defend a wrongful termination, and also cost the employer in lost productivity, poor morale among staff, and lost reputation for an unlawful action.

Key elements in a termination should include performance evaluation records, disciplinary action, and attendance. The employer should also consider other similarly-situated staff, and how they were treated or coached through similar situations. If the separated employee is being treated differently from others, and faces the adverse employment action of termination, the employer might be creating fertile ground for a lawsuit.

If there is an inconsistency in how an employer treated a terminated employee at the point of termination, the ex-employee can quickly become a complainant who hires an attorney to review all records for the employee, and for the department. Many employers fall into the trap of thinking "at will" employment means a staff member can be fired at will. In theory this is true; however, mistreatment or discrimination is not authorized in any state.

Adrienne Foxhall was very excited about her new position. After completing her master's degree at Vanderbilt, she moved to Charlotte, North Carolina to accept a Director of Leadership and Training position in the medical center, paying just over $85,000. She quickly purchased a condo in the northern suburbs, and decided to trade in her beat up Honda for a new hybrid.

In her new job, Adrienne had six staff reporting to her. Her department was developing workshops and training opportunities for medical personnel in the region. Her position reported to the Vice President of Educational Initiatives, Porter Bestt. Adrienne Foxhall was an African-American woman in her late 20s, from the poorest part of South Carolina. Her mother had finished high school, and her dad had finished his associates' degree. She had six other brothers and sisters, and typically sent money back home. Not only was she the first in her family to get a college degree, she was the first to get a master's and leave South Carolina. She had scraped and worked hard to get through Vanderbilt, earning spending money in addition to the full academic scholarship she had won. Her parents were so proud of her, but she refused to go back for long periods of time. Her hope was to prosper in Charlotte, perhaps settle down, and get married.

At first she was excited about her new boss, Porter Bestt. Porter was a Duke graduate who had developed the Educational Initiative Sector. He had written a few white papers, published an article, and presented at national conventions. Adrienne originally thought she could learn a great deal from Porter.

What Adrienne learned in the first two months was that Porter had a staff favorite, Victoria. Victoria was a young white female, athletic, and a former gymnast. Some thought she was cute. But Victoria was a "kiss ass" and constant complainer. The rest of the staff could not stand her and refused to reveal personal information because they all knew she ran back to Porter. Porter was a smart man; what he didn't have from a formal education, he often had in common sense and business acumen. But somehow he was a horrible supervisor. He was more interested in talking about Super Bowl parties and his speed boat, than discussing any initiatives or goals for the office.

Adrienne became beleaguered, fielding the constant complaints about Victoria, how Victoria flirted with one of the clients. Victoria had a reputation for sleeping with the Administrative Assistant in the annex. But Adrienne couldn't do anything about it as Victoria was Porter's pet. Adrienne found that the staff soon lost faith in her, as they thought she could clean up Victoria's sexual Aegean stables, so to speak. Instead, Adrienne found herself strategizing mentally. She had to survive this job, though she had no support from her boss and no support at home. She sought a long time mentor, and was devising plans to stay in place while Porter continued on about inappropriate personal business. Meanwhile, Victoria was a wet spot left to roam the administrative countryside with her beguiling ways.

Adrienne's mentor suggested that she start setting goals for her staff meetings with Porter. Since Porter could not stay focused, or even provide any support after Adrienne's constant requests for help, Adrienne sought support on how to hold her staff together and provide effective evaluations without the emotional interjections from Porter. Porter's idea of an evaluation was to talk about how 'happy" Victoria was, or how she developed a funny PowerPoint slideshow about movies and TV shows to help morale. All Adrienne could think was, "These activities are not part of anyone's job description."

Over the course of a year, Adrienne and Porter drifted apart. Adrienne didn't think she was hired to be Porter's friend and social counselor. Drinking with the boss after work, or hanging out in the morning, was not her idea of a professional relationship. Adrienne wanted a boss who would teach her something professionally, not play favorites with the staff slut and constantly give unfair criticism to Adrienne based on cavalier remarks from a very young staff, which was enduring constant turnover under Porter. The only thing that kept Adrienne encouraged was that she did receive two bonuses for her sixth and twelve months of service. She had signed seven new contracts for training, and received the positive attention of the medical staff who appreciated her mature yet ebullient training style.

The issue that made Adrienne emerge from her quiet stance was Victoria's inappropriate and foul mouthed complaining in an open meeting, about how the staff did not get along. She continued for a solid ten minutes about how it was a tough place to work, no one got along. Victoria actually had the nerve to hurl a few barbs at Adrienne in the process. The looks on the staffs' faces — disgust, disengagement — Adrienne had to end the meeting.

As staff paraded out quickly, she called Victoria back.

"I am concerned here, Victoria. There was no need to rip up the staff, and use that kind of language. I know you are friends with Porter, and that is fine. Did you ever consider that your friendship with Porter might be part of the reason staff don't trust you?" Adrienne was more candid than she had planned, but it was the truth.

Victoria countered, "Adrienne, you know I am just upset. I don't get it. The gossip around here is unreal. We needed you to come and do something different and…"

Adrienne cut her off, "And? What are you saying? What I am saying is that your friendship with Porter is divisive. You misuse it all the time and people are tired of it."

Adrienne paused, "Maybe I am being naïve, but I think it would go a long way if you could take this constructive criticism and reflect on it, think about how you fit in here."

Victoria obviously was not taking it well. Her eyes were big as saucers, and her face was red. She couldn't believe she was being checked.

Adrienne hadn't second guessed what she said. She was the director of the office. She should be able to coach and caution staff as needed. No one wanted Victoria around, and no one appreciated her flirtatious friendship with the Vice President, but no one said a thing and the office morale was horrible. How could her office train others, if they can't get along themselves?

Two days later, Adrienne was called into a last-minute meeting with the Vice President, Porter Bestt. She also noted the director of Human Resources was present. She figured this was to discuss Victoria.

Porter started, "I heard about what you did with Victoria."

Adrienne understood what this was about. "She is out of control. No one supports…"

Porter cut her off, "You have no place giving her the stay-in-your-place talk! I thought you people more than anyone would understand that!

Adrienne was shocked "You people?"

"I have warned you before about the staff; they need to be able to come to me."

"I have encouraged them, and I have also talked about how I feel undercut by her. The morale is low, the…"

"I can't have you doing this, Adrienne. We have enough problems with turnover. People will leave if we keep you on…"

"What? No one has left since I have been here."

"We are afraid they will. I didn't bring you here from Vanderbilt to do this. You have no one to blame but yourself."

The HR director saw the meeting spiraling out of control. The director touched Porter's arm and paused for a moment.

Porter composed himself and continued, "Well, it isn't about any of this anyway, we are off track. I know you have done some hard work. You have made great strides trying to work through staff morale, and have brought us four new clients, but I have to talk to you about our organization."

"We are conducting a few of these meetings this month. Our revenue across the organization is down 15%. When I hired you I was optimistic, but we just can't sustain a director's position now."

Adrienne protested a bit, "But I asked these questions at the interview and you assured me that this was not the case."

The director of Human Resources interrupted, "Yes, we did project an upward trend in a number of areas, but that just didn't happen."

Adrienne couldn't believe it; she was being fired after twelve months and two bonuses.

The director of Human Resources continued, "It's a business necessity. We would have to lay off two of your staff to make up your salary. Porter is going to take on all your duties for the rest of the year and give us a chance to reevaluate."

The director paused and let the information seep in, "So Adrienne, this is Tuesday, we can give you Wednesday and Thursday off, and you can come back and we will throw you a little party to say goodbye to staff and colleagues if you like. Here is a severance package, too. You weren't with us long, but you did good work."

Adrienne had no intention of attending some little party to celebrate being laid off, and HR knew it. It was a nice gesture, but an empty one. The severance package was standard: a release from a legal complaint, a noncompete clause, and confidentiality statements. The severance gave Adrienne six weeks to regroup and moving expenses of $2500.

The HR director looked at Adrienne kindly, while Porter was staring out the window. "I'm sorry Adrienne, but we will give you good references."

Adrienne knew the market was tough. She didn't want to be a fighter, anyway. She was given a small parachute and a chance to go back and find another job with a boss who would appreciate her. She wished she had a chance to talk with her attorney.

Adrienne paused, then commented, "I won't want a party or anything, I will just get my things tomorrow evening if that is ok? I'll bring this signed severance form back as well. This is a lot to digest right now. I want to look over it."

The HR director seemed flustered. Porter was edgy too, when Adrienne asked for more time to sign the severance package. "Sure, here is my card with my direct number. If you want to pull any files off your email, you will have remote access for the next 48 hours. We typically don't do that, but you have been a good employee." She paused again. "I do need to collect your keys and ID when you return, as well."

Adrienne sighed. She wasn't happy, but the severance pay would help. She would have health benefits for another six months, and references. She had a chance to reset her career after a bad fit. She stood and extended her hand to HR. "We'll see you tomorrow."

Adrienne looked at Porter, "Guess, this is good bye."

Porter was stiff, but still extended his hand, "Good luck. You do have talent, Adrienne. Be sure to wrap everything up with HR so we can do the necessary paperwork to get your package in order."

Adrienne, still feeling stunned, did recall the organization was facing cuts in other areas. She was the newest hired. It stung, but in these economic times, at least she had a year and a half service and references. On the way home, she stopped for takeout Italian, lasagna and garlic bread, her favorite comfort food. She also got a bottle of merlot. Might as well chill out and prepare for the next step.

After sleeping in until 9am, something she had not done in years, Adrienne looked around her condo and imagined the hassle of moving. She had a few things from her office stacked by the door, and that severance agreement. She read over it again. Something just didn't feel right.

Initially, she was going to move her things back to Tennessee. Her graduate school professors were supportive; she could make some inroads there, but she certainly wasn't going back to South Carolina. That afternoon, Adrienne was out at the local pizza shop. She was a mess, wearing glasses, baggy pants, with her hair crammed in a Vanderbilt hat. She ran into her old assistant.

"Hi Adrienne, I... I... Her assistant hugged her, "I can't say how sorry I am."

Adrienne was startled, and wished she didn't run into her.

"It all happened so fast, I've meant to call you, but...

Adrienne looked up, "Hey, I had no support at all. I'm gonna just make other plans."

Adrienne's assistant handed her a business card, "Well, while you are making plans, check him out. I called him, so he will talk to you briefly. Adrienne, you have a case."

The thought did cross her mind while she was kicking back that bottle of merlot last night, but she wanted to just move on and think about it later.

"Adrienne, you were the best Director that place ever saw. You are talented, and they just couldn't handle you. Porter was threatened by you from the beginning. You have a case."

Adrienne hugged her former assistant, "Thanks, I'll think about it."

Adrienne did call the employment attorney, who agreed to meet her the following morning. After hearing the story of favoritism and even sexism, he agreed to take the case on contingency. She claimed race discrimination as they favored Victoria. Porter had used gossip and hearsay to separate Adrienne, not a documented appraisal. Adrienne had no evaluations or progressive discipline, only bonuses.

Adrienne was smart. She had paused before signing that severance agreement which would have eliminated her option to sue the employer. Her bosses made a critical error at the termination meeting complaining about how Adrienne treated a subordinate, who was obviously acting out.

Favoritism for a white employee made the case colorable. Adrienne's case was supported by her performance and bonuses. The employer tried using the term "business necessity" to show that it wasn't personal, racial or any other prejudice. However, Porter was obviously motivated by Adrienne admonishing Victoria.

Adrienne was disheartened by her job loss. She was only doing her job by discussing inappropriate behavior with a subordinate. Instead of working with her as the director of the office, Porter sided with his pet, Victoria, and had Adrienne terminated. Adrienne had complained about Victoria and the lack of support during her employment. She made verbal complaints about how she was treated. Adrienne filed her case in federal court. She claimed disparate treatment based on race. She had exercised her organizational right as director to coach and admonish a staff member. Apparently, this led to her unlawful termination.

In its defense, the medical center took Adrienne through several interrogatories and requests for discovery. Over a six month period, she had to sign waivers for them to investigate her face book page, all tweets, cell phone records, and text messages. Even her medical and gynecological records were fodder for examination as she claimed emotional distress.

As the case grew to a head under the mountains of paper traded by plaintiff and defendant, Adrienne was subjected to a two and a half day deposition. The first series of questions related to her family life. She was accused of being racist herself since she emerged from an all black school district in South Carolina. Next her work history was questioned. She found herself defending three days she took off to have a cyst removed. Also, she had requests for jury duty in a two year period. The defendant believed Adrienne made up these excuses to get extra vacation days. Adrienne found herself requesting those documents from the courthouse to prove she indeed served on two different juries during that time period.

Her brother's alcoholism was thrown in her face. The medical school's attorney tried to establish that alcoholism ran in the family; and it was this behavior that made Adrienne an unsavory employee. Throughout the humiliating questions, Adrienne kept her cool. She prayed briefly during the breaks. She had a massage at the end of day one to relax. She stayed grounded and focused for the duration.

After scrubbing her records to uncover her gynecological records, travel on her car, and the books she was reading, and the deposition concluded. Her attorney of course sat with her through the whole ordeal. She had learned his style regarding what he would object to, and what was an unfair question, and was pleased with his focus and professional demeanor.

In conclusion he stated, "Adrienne, you did well. I know it was a grueling couple of days. But I am pleased with your answers. You remained calm and poised. I am sure they don't want someone like you on the stand."

Adrienne nodded "But they have set the pre-trial hearing for five weeks from now. These don't usually go to court, but I have to be prepared."

Adrienne responded, "Thanks, I am ready for a merlot." She headed off and reflected on the stress of the last few days. She was still standing, and confident in her answers. She had nothing to hide. Truth was on her side.

She had to sit and wait for the defendants to deliberate on how to cover their tracks from discriminatory action. She knew patience was a virtue here. Ten business days later, Adrienne's attorney called. Adrienne had learned over the past year that life goes on. Her attorney said that they didn't want to go to trial. The defendant's motion to dismiss was denied. The medical center saw that they should consider settling instead of engaging in expensive court costs. After 19 months, Adrienne was awarded a year's salary and a year of health benefits. The medical center had already spent close to $45,000 in legal fees. Going to court would skyrocket the costs. Adrienne, who had found a job 8 months after her termination, had mitigated some of the employment loss damages. She could never recoup lost retirement, or deaden the humiliation of being fired. Nonetheless, she had emerged a victor. Her lesson was to carefully research the organization and employer before taking a job. She discovered that most of the people they terminated were people of color. Two others had brought lawsuits against the medical center.

From the employer's point of view, it was believable in a recession that an $85,000 salary could be needed to recoup financial losses. Porter could have easily absorbed Adrienne's duties for several months to clear up any suspicion of wrongful termination. The Human Resources Director tried to smooth things over, giving Adrienne respect and support for her transition and $15,000 in the severance package. However, Porter had already offered up his complaint of unfair treatment of white employees, of personal hearsay, or other emotional rationale an employer might tell an employee to justify termination. The term business necessity meant it wasn't personal, racial or due to any other prejudice, but in Adrienne's case, it was used as an excuse to eliminate Adrienne's employment. Clearly, Porter was motivated to protect his pet, Victoria. However, the separation meeting was critical in setting the stage for how Adrienne felt and later moved to seek an attorney. Adrienne took a necessary pause instead of signing away her right to sue; she denied her employer the "get out of jail free card." The employer's mistake in acting emotionally and in haste resulted in high turnover within the department after Adrienne was unfairly terminated. The medical center also had to pay costly court expenses.

Chapter 11

"Do I really want to be integrated into a burning house?" Advice to complainants

Close to 50 years later, James Baldwin" question is relevant. Perhaps the questions are shocking to ask, as we have supposedly made so much progress. If you pull yourself up by your boot straps, you can attend those private schools, lead a charmed life nestled along a tree lined drive. You can even become president of the United States. But can you work day in and day out as Jack Ordinary, simply trying to make a way for his family? Or, does the presence of the people emerging from the margins pose too great a threat to mainstream society that retaliatory actions of employers had climbed to record levels in 2009 and again in 2010.

These remarks in this final chapter are a compilation of common themes that complainants mentioned as they discussed their respective cases. These comments are not an attempt at providing legal advice, or even statistically significant findings which could guide someone's actions if he or she is contemplating filing an EEOC complaint. Nonetheless, many of these remarks have merit for the strong-willed, for those willing to reflect on next steps, or those considering walking away. Given one's perspective in life, all options hold merit. Enduring the fangs of discrimination as it has a deleterious effect on one's career and personal life is enough to make even the strongest-willed person pause.

1. Wait to file, but don't wait too long.

In a few cases, the women presented in this volume knew at the instant of separation that the employer was wrong. The possibility of filing is open immediately. However, an employer bold enough and cavalier enough to break federal rules is often uninformed enough to continue this trend, hence potentially proving the case for discrimination. I don't at all suggest waiting six months for the case to run stale; however, waiting even two or three months can allow an employer to become comfortable and continue the discriminatory behavior, providing more crucial evidence.

For example, one of the women, Valencia Jones was terminated from her executive administrative position with no warning, no coaching, and no write up, no indication that there was a problem, except one heated exchange with her boss three weeks previous to the termination. She had 30 years' experience, two masters' degrees, a doctorate, and various certifications, and she served as a national officer of her discipline's organization. Perhaps this was part of the problem "Too black, too strong." Valencia Jones commented during our interview that she felt as if she were enduring an out of body experience, as if she was watching from the curb as her own career was enduring a head-on collision. She simply returned to her office quietly and gathered a few items. It appeared to her staff that she had walked off the job until she returned the following term as a tenured faculty member.

In another story, Kansas Ogilvie's termination happened right before a holiday, so she had time to reflect on next steps. Should she go back to school, travel the world, have another child? Maybe she should enter civic work? The shock lingered, and she was reminded that she did work in an at-will state. A month went by. The same people who were shocked by her sudden departure called her with other tidbits; other African Americans and Hispanics were leaving the institution. In fact, if there were twelve people of color, eight left. Kansas Ogilvie served as a reference for some people of color who were taking lower-paying jobs or demotions at another organization, just to leave a systemically discriminatory environment. Kansas Ogilvie's husband was beside himself, as he saw his wife climb her career ladder only to endure this unexpected shock; but he also advised her to move on as he had a hard time dealing with the injustice.

Three and a half months later, she learned that her former boss had hired a white female, with half the experience, half the credentials, almost half her age but earning double the salary. The new hire was rumored to be well connected with friends in the company; her father attended the same schools as the company executive, even presented together at regional conferences. Kansas Ogilvie had been pushed out to make room for someone's friend, at the expense of her own career. In fact, most of the people of color who left were replaced by Caucasians, less qualified Caucasians. All the people of color who left were highly qualified, with multiple certifications, double masters' and various degrees from Ivy League schools, state schools, and good schools with solid reputations. Yet their own education did not provide a protective hedge in this racist environment.

In another example, Raquel Battle collected her documents, emails, and files. She also brought copies on a USB key for the attorney to keep. All this was topped off by her resume so the attorney could see she was not some opportunist, but a smart woman who is well trained analytically. In front of two attorneys, a paralegal and a secretary, Raquel spilled her story of discrimination, and without tears or anxiety. She answered the attorney's questions and clarified the time line. After two hours and 15 minutes, the attorney agreed to take the case on contingency.

During her three month wait, her previous employer had made several colorable decisions, hiring all whites in the wake of a black and Hispanic exodus. They never replaced the diversity officer who left abruptly, and did not follow their own policies. Further, as other people of color left, they willingly made statements incriminating of the former employer. They were leaving for the same reason that Raquel was fired; systemic racism prevailed.

Proving a racial discrimination case is Herculean task; it can feel like cleaning out the Aegean stables, cutting though an organization's posturing and hypocrisy. Though waiting was not a strategy, Kansas Ogilvie's, Raquel Battle's, and Valencia Jones' delays played in their favor. The delay in filing allowed all of their former bosses to get comfortable and continue the pattern of racism. Other staff, once they recovered from the shock of their abrupt terminations, provided assistance and statements that supported her case. In fact, their resignations were timely. Time passing put the organization on its heels, flat footed almost. By the time all three women had filed their cases, people had resigned, and the decisions to replace people of color with all whites had already been made.

It is never simple. Between filing a case and getting any organization to the table takes 30 days for them to respond with "we didn't do it." Then, the attorneys must go before a judge and repeat the antics. "Yes you did it" "No we didn't......... na na nananana!" If one files with the EEOC, the same exchange of 'yes-you-did...no-we-didn't' goes on through the mail. The process will try anyone's nerves, put the complainant in the position of living and reliving the situations to explain to the attorneys repeatedly what happened. Careers and families are short circuited. By the time the court case is filed, or the EEOC investigation starts, the personal damage to the complainant has already been put in motion.

2. Keep confidences. Loose lips sink cases.

The complainant will find the most unlikely compatriots in his or her fight for justice. One interviewer commented about how she was allowed to sit in on a conciliation hearing of a fellow complainant. It allowed her to prepare for her own meeting with the same organization. Some colleagues will grow a huge conscience and offer to participate in the investigation, or point an investigator in the right direction. Don't betray such trust by giving up their identities. Once they are revealed, even to an attorney, you have compromised them and jeopardized your own flow of information.

Two of the complainants commented on how the most unsuspecting white men came to their aid. At the risk of sounding stereotypical, Kansas Ogilvie commented, "I could not believe this rosy white-haired man came to my defense!" While a good provider to his wife and grown children, this unsuspecting white man made more phone calls, and wrote more letters to Human Resources in defense of Kansas than anyone. Her surprise was intensified even more with the knowledge that she had verbally reprimanded him the month previous for tardiness. Kansas came to rely on this white man who served as a major witness in her internal and external investigation. He even took her to lunch after her termination to assure her that she was talented and would find another job.

When she asked why he came to the rescue, he said, "It was the right thing just like it was the right thing for you to tell me I was late. You could have let me continue and fired me. Instead you were honest. I am just being honest. That is the only right thing to do."

"It takes a village to file a complaint," one of the complainants described. In her situation, one of her colleagues had walked off the job only three weeks before. This colleague was in the midst of determining a severance package, for a pittance of course. But for the company, this was key because every severance package typically has a nondisclosure clause, a confidentiality clause, and all kinds of other legalese that will keep people from telling a third party where the bodies are buried. The complainant retells how her colleague gave up the severance to avoid the confidentiality clause, so she could support the complainant's bigger claim of discrimination. Her colleague forfeited her own severance to support the complainant's discrimination charge. The complainant realized then she had to fight. She was given the baton of racial and gender equality to carry, and while it would bruise her knees to clear those hurdles, she realized she was not running alone, and not running for just herself.

3. Turncoat alert: be braced for the unlikely coward

One of the women I interviewed, who I'll refer to as Caprice, shared several points that were mirrored some of the other cases of discrimination. If people look around at their staff, they might imagine the one who will step up, step forward to fight with you. The old saying, "Don't judge a book by its cover" applies. In a comical manner, Caprice recalled the administrative assistant on her job. They called him Seymour X. He was a gay male who was very clear about his sexuality, his husband, and his place in society as a marginalized citizen from the gay community. He was an interesting mix of militant Nation of Islam, and Stonewall rights. It's ironic how these two ideologies can manifest themselves into one character. And he was a character, a caricature that one could always count on to fight the establishment. He had lost his parents because of his sexual orientation, and his brother to a car accident. He was a fighter in many ways, edgy, smart, a presumed confidant over troubled waters — or so one thought.

He was so upset! How they could do this to a SISTA! She had done so much for him and the other people of color. She was like superwoman, if superwoman could be Angela Bassett. He was so distraught, he said "Girl don't let them take your invisible plane. You gotta fight — fight the powa! I will come over and watch *Do the Right Thing* and we are gonna strategize. We will fight them!"

Caprice was humbled that someone appeared to care that much about her plight. She too was stunned, but had spent two or three days crying alone in her apartment, wondering if she had to move back east with her aunt to get by. And Seymour did come by with his husband, Dwayne. They watched the Spike Lee Joint, drank some martinis and bitched about work. They even cried together. Caprice felt reassured that filing a complaint with the Human Relations Commission of her state was the thing to do. She had complained about her own civil rights, about being harassed racially and sexually by the boss, then was terminated only a month later, with her employer saying it was performance-related. "Performance my ass!" said Seymour. "Our numbers neva looked this good, not before you! Our boss, well, he just wanted a little pie with that cake. He never thought your bakery would be closed." Seymour was too much, but just the right blend of anger and spite to get her to muster up her courage to move on this. Her uncle told her, "Walk away, this ain't the lunch counter. Get on with your life." Her father had the same sentiment, "Do you know you will spend two to three years reliving this? You were looking to leave any way."

Caprice gathered her records and witness list to go to the Commission. She had dates, pay stubs, and stats; the intake person marveled at the blatant nature of the case. "I can't comment, but Caprice, I see this every day. It is a shame how people treat each other."

Caprice did find another job, as her investigation went on. She sent in more papers, set the conciliation meeting through the commission; she was hurt and scared, but she knew this was the fight. As she entered the commission on the day of her meeting, the investigator met her, "I have to talk to you ma'am. About your case."

The investigator called her 'Ma'am' So formal, what was going on?

"Your key witness withdrew, Seymour something or other. All he said was he knew you were right. But he could not risk his job. He's sorry."

Caprice was beside herself; whatever happened to this "fight the power!" What happened to solidarity?

Her conciliation meeting continued, and the basics of the case were solid. Her charges of discrimination, sexual harassment and retaliation were so clear, Ray Charles could see it. She exercised her civil rights, and then she was fired. A case is never open and shut, but two years and four months later, she got half of the possible back pay. Between taxes, her scrambling to work other jobs and a major detour in her career, her options boiled down to "keep everyone from court." It was bittersweet — more bitter than sweet as her acquaintances and social circles had changed. She was less visible; she stopped going to church. She was tired of people asking about her career. She had no kids or husband. It was always about her career.

The commission and former employer spent another two months hashing out the settlement language. Nuances of confidentiality, reliability, past practice, statements of culpability were all jumbled up in phone calls, faxes, and email attachments. Right before it was all over she did receive a card from Seymour, who had stopped calling and didn't return her calls. She took the hint.

The card read, "So sorry. You know Dwayne couldn't bear another case. We just went through fighting for same sex rights on his job. I knew you would prevail... X!"

He still had the nerve to sign it "X."

Other complainants had similar stories; coworkers who had corroborating cases, but walked away. People stopped talking to them. Don't waste time dwelling on those with less determination or commitment. Everyone is not Nat Turner, or Dorothy Height, and everyone can't be. In retrospect, perhaps it is this very mild tenor and behavior that allows discriminatory people to overlook them as these personalities pose little threat. While the complainant might not respect it, respect that being mild and under the radar is indeed a protective strategy, even if it is unconscious.

4. Pariah Effect

Have you ever watched a sitcom, where some poor dupe is walking around with a "KICK ME" sign on his back and doesn't know it? People avoid him, and talk about the poor fool behind his back. No one sits with him at lunch. He is the last person people sit next to at meetings. While I am trying to bring levity to the situation, this can be your experience if you are a complainant who retains his or her job in the midst of a legal action or EEOC complaint. Many employers (but not all) will recognize that once someone files a complaint, any adverse action afterwards only ups the ante for the complainant. For example, Mary complains of sexual harassment and she is demoted; the employer can be tagged with retaliation. Mary complains, and then her employers transfer her to a remote office.... retaliation. Mary complains and then her shift changes; this action can be construed as retaliation. Mary is a hot potato, and seldom do people want to be around when the music stops.

Sondra Wilson commented that before she complained, people were willing to align with her as the martyr. Everyone saw the mistreatment she endured, and admired her for trying to hang in there until retirement. As long as she was the whipping post, the boss left the others alone. Her colleagues and friends silently supported her while she endured harassing comments in meetings and "misunderstandings," such as her parking spot getting moved across campus, and having the locks changed on her office with no one telling her. Under this new management, the organization was more aggressive. Her new boss stepped up the pressure, leaving her no choice but to go to the EEOC only months before her planned retirement.

Once her organization learned of her complaint, that KICK ME sign went on. However, in sitcoms, the duped party doesn't know; in real life, the complainant is fully aware of being ostracized. For Sondra in this case, people stopped making eye contact with her, even in passing. She used to meet with a group of ladies for lunch once a month; that little outing soon became chocked full of excuses and they stopped coming. They would not even be seen with her after work, though their kids used to play together. Aliza Rojas mentioned that people would not speak to her at the bus stop, but miles from campus would apologize quietly for not speaking. They would say, "I just can't risk getting into trouble at work." Many were ashamed but desperate for their jobs.

Complainants found that some people in their own families wanted them to walk away from the fight. Valencia Jones was shocked when she got a panicked call from her cousin asking her to drop the whole thing.

He said, "I am getting the cold shoulder on my job."

"C'mon," Val said, "this is a big town. It might be your cheap cologne or the gas you pass after you have milk at lunch."

"I am serious Val! Drop it! It is hurting us."

Val was shocked. She was being asked to give up the fight, by her own family. She just stopped talking about it. She learned like many complainants, if you are going to fight this fight, gather around the most positive people, those who really support your trials. Enough people will view you with that KICK ME sign on your back; your own inner circle for this process should be confident and positive, even if you face a setback.

It is OK to love people from afar while you are in this fight, but be sure to fight with those who won't remind you of the KICK ME sign on your back. As a complainant, your employer has already heeded the sign.

5. It ain't over til it's over — defendants' mechanism

A few of the complainants found that their defending employers would resort to unethical tactics in an attempt to force an early settlement. Defendants often know they're wrong; further, defendants know that the cost of litigation and defense can be astronomical. In short, the defending company has every motive to coerce a complainant to drop the case or take an early settlement.

Sondra Wilson had filed a racial discrimination case against her employer. She had racist emails and minutes from meetings in which women were talked about in disparaging ways. Her case was strong, but the EEOC investigation was dragging on. During the same timeframe, her organization was facing an audit from a regulatory agency regarding financial practices. The audit included a thorough review of all records, books, and several middle level staff. While Sondra Wilson had negligible interaction with the financial end of the district, somehow she found herself under severe scrutiny for financial impropriety. Her district was naming her as the primary reason for the problems, though there were no records to prove it.

Sondra had no choice but to file a second complaint with her employment attorney to review the files and charges. After four weeks of her own attorney-led investigation, it was made plain that her organization had tried to frame Sondra in an effort to get her to drop her original charges. They had uncovered files and forms that had Sondra Wilson's signature, though it didn't match. The crucial evidence was a set of directives and memos signed by Sondra, but held signatures dated when she was out for a three-day outpatient procedure. Her district was playing hardball. In an attempt to smear Sondra, the defending employer ended up with a retaliation charge added to Sondra's original charge.

Valencia Jones also had problems with her defending employer during the investigation. She discovered that her home email had been hacked, and her work email was being monitored regularly. An organization does have the right to review email that goes through its server, if it is treating everyone the same. By singling out Valencia's email and phone, the defending organization engaged in another adverse action on the job; and Valencia filed a second complaint of harassment.

In both of these examples, defending employers made attempts to weaken the resolve of the complainant, or put them in a position to ask for the defending employer's help. If anything negative happens after the initial complaint is filed, review it with an HRC or attorney. Be sure to act quickly to uncover any possible wrongdoing on behalf of the defending employer.

6. Human Relations or Lawyers?

If a complainant decides to file, there are two options: 1) go straight to an attorney or 2) go to the local or regional Human Rights Office or EEOC to file.

Option 1 — The attorney. The attorney may or may not take your case on contingency. If he takes it on contingency, you must have a strong case, as no attorney (on any case for that matter) will work on something that will not bear profit. With that said, an attorney wants to win, and win as quickly as possible with the highest possible yield. Remember he earns one-third of your settlement. A solid employment attorney is trained to field these cases and provide you with timely support as your case evolves. There could be a court filing, which means that your discrimination case becomes a matter of public record. You may face hearings, dispositions, and other meetings, but the attorney sometimes moves more quickly than Option 2.

Option 2 — A Human Relations/Rights Commission (HRC). In the experiences of the women interviewed, the HRC is a state or federal run agency. They are indeed goodhearted people who are in this business because they often believe in equality. Translation: they don't necessarily believe in making a lot of money; they believe in the greater good. In this case, the greater good is packaged in a language employers understand, monetary loss. Often the greater good takes more time and is on a budget. Many of these agencies and commissions are swamped. Do the math, as state and federal governments are issuing cutbacks, EEOC cases have skyrocketed. In short, they have fewer people to process more complaints. The HRC can work to settle these matters quietly, without it getting filed formally in court. But this can require several calls from you for updates. Persistence and patience is the name of the game. They are not on your side or against you; they are there to uphold the law. But you have to help them. Some organizations will settle with an HRC. Others will force you to wait out the situation until you get a Right to Sue Letter at the end of the first year. Then the complainant can be thrown right back to Option 1, get an attorney.

The benefit of starting with an HRC and moving to an attorney is that a significant part of the discovery and research is done by the time you get that

Right to Sue Letter. If you are patient, this drives down attorney costs. And also, if a complainant receives a Right to Sue Letter from an HRC or EEOC, many attorneys will take the case on contingency. Finally, an HRC may settle the case for you, and you find yourself not even needing to go to Option 1, the attorney. Forty percent of the women interviewed had their cases settled by an HRC/EEOC unit without retaining an attorney.

The salient question is…. ***How patient are you?***

If there is a large amount at stake (that is your back pay exceeds $50,000) you may need an attorney to strong arm the defending organization. The standard attorney fee is one-third of your settlement. Remember, though: 67% of something is better than 100% of nothing. Don't expect a trial. Eliminate the images of Tom Cruise or Gene Hackman thundering away at your boss in open court, calling them a racist or sexist pig in front of God and country. We see that in movies because it is entertainment. Almost none of these cases ever see a court room. The minuscule number that actually arrive at the courthouse seldom go to trial, as a case with this type of strength often gets settled. Instead expect conciliations, meetings, and long drawn-out discussions over settlement language. You can win, it will cost you a pound of flesh, but you will probably not win what the court will allow, nor do you probably want to spend your life (and it does eat up your life) enduring this emotional rollercoaster for 2-3 years.

No matter which option you take, the attorney or the HRC on the way to the attorney, whichever you chose, wear alligator skin and get on with your life while you are fighting this. And no matter which option you choose, be polite. Your attorney and the HRC staff are working for you not against you. Don't take out your frustrations in a very difficult situation on the very people who are signed on to be in your corner. And in your frustration, note that either option takes more than a year, in most cases.

7. How to choose an attorney

When going to battle, be more strategic than choosing up sides at your company's pick-up softball game. You want to truly consider who you are fighting and who might be best-suited to fight for you. For example, if you emerge from higher education, do your research and find attorneys who have fought higher education institutions, and know the difference between tenure, adjunct, part-time and regular full-time. If you are a union member, try to find an attorney who has dealt with unions and knows the nuances of these organizations. If you are emerging from health or pharmacy, try to find an attorney who is conversant with those medical environments, and has proven success fighting in those environments.

Consider who you are fighting. Attorneys belong to the same bar association, they go to lunch together, and go to the same health clubs sometimes. Yes, they are bound by confidentiality, but both parties are tasked with concluding the case. If you are fighting a large organization, try to choose an attorney who would be slightly outside of the proximity. One complainant was fighting a large organization in Chicago, Illinois. She had a hard time finding an attorney who would take on such a case. Her ace in the hole came through a medium-sized firm that wanted to make a name for itself. She found them through a referral of a good friend who had dealt with them previously. Once she won her case, several other people approached her about her attorney. The word of mouth system is often the best way to find a good attorney.

You want to consider an attorney's track record, and even their place of business. If you hired someone who is working out of a shack on the seedy side of town, the other attorneys know your seedy attorney is potentially desperate, perhaps quicker to make a deal, or just isn't the sharpest pencil in the box. If you choose an attorney who has years of service, various decisions in their favor and a good work environment, you would know this attorney is making not just enough for his or her overhead, but to more than enough to maintain his or her style of living. He or she is a winner — just what you want.

You should interview them just as they interview you. Look at their past cases, find out about their track record. Also remember, you are not shopping for a friend, but a legal shark. This attorney doesn't have to have personal warmth, hold your hand, and offer you tissues as you spill out your story. He or she does have to be analytical, strategic and somewhat aggressive. Remember all those unsavory jokes about attorneys being heartless and conniving and never getting into heaven, those qualities are useful when you go to battle. Of course you want an ethical attorney, but remember, you want a winner, not a social worker.

8. Dollars and sense

Often complainants and defendants wonder about the cost of these cases. The cost to the complainant is up front, lost salary, and the losses that occur when bills are not paid. Complainants can become desperate quickly, especially in a weak economy. Often employers prey on the desperation of complainants and try to throw nominal money at the case to produce an early settlement. Do not cash any checks, sign anything, or receive anything your defending employer sends you directly without the advice of the EEOC or your attorney, if you have one. Employers have been known to work around the attorney and send a nominal amount in the mail, for past health, retirement, or other severance issues. If the complainant in desperation signs for these items, and/or cashes the check, he or she could be unwittingly signing over further rights to pursue litigation. Check with the EEOC or your attorney before signing anything. Past employers may send such temptations to test the mettle and resilience of the complainant.

Complainants who had savings and family support were able to weather the financial storm in their lives. One complainant specifically stated that she had witnessed the lengthy proceeding when her brother fought his past employer. And he did settle, almost two years later. However, he only had one job. He had nothing to help him through financially. He lost his condominium; his car was repossessed, and he ended up living with mom for a year before he could get on his feet. His credit was devastated, as he couldn't sell his condo fast enough before the bank put it in foreclosure. After living with mom for a few months, he lost his fiancée. The settlement was nice, but his life changed forever. From watching his troubles, the complainant swore always to keep multiple revenue streams. She did some consulting for an organization, worked part time for an accountant in the spring of each year, and taught classes at the community college. "It's a po' rat that has only one hole to go to." She admits it wasn't sexy, but when adverse action came calling for her, she could maintain and wait out the company for all that was truly due her.

Companies and organizations often don't consider the costs of defending an EEOC charge. As one attorney puts it "Any fool can sue you." Attorneys' fees now are anywhere from $250 to $450/hour, depending on your region of the country. The urban area attorneys are more expensive. A single EEOC charge against an organization can cost $450/hour in attorney fees, and can easily soar to $20,000 and more to defend. Often large companies carry liability insurance to help offset nuisance complaints and other legal issues for small to medium companies; such a charge can be devastating. A finding of even $25,000 can ruin the small business owner and force him or her into bankruptcy. Proper training, and preventative measures by the employer, are the best way to offset these complaints. The best offense for a company is a good defense. The figures below are cursory settlement numbers for credible cases. Remember settlement numbers are tied directly to the complainant's salary at the time of forced separation.

- $10K- $20K- If settled at initial point of filing (settled within six months)
- $50K- $120K- If case settled at conciliation, mediation or other pretrial procedure (perhaps 9 – 18 months later)
- $185K- If settled once trial has started (Perhaps two- three years later)
- $250K- If plaintiff wins court case – PLUS when the case goes to trial, the court also awards the attorney fees which can easily exceed another $100,000.

These numbers only summarize the monetary losses. The losses in reputation for the employer, and sometimes the complainant, have no tangible measure.

9. Don't hate your brother of another mother

It is easy to fall into a cycle of hate when you have faced racial or sexual discrimination. Some of the cases were so blatant and surreal, I could not believe some of the details revealed in interviewing complainants. In many ways I felt bad asking these women to relive their experiences for this project. The worst of humanity can be found in racial- and sexually-driven cases.

Racial and sexual discrimination cases often involved the insecurities, and / or hatred of a person in power who adversely affects someone trying to do a good job. And no single race or gender is immune. Women discriminate against men, blacks and Hispanics discriminate against whites. And we all suffer as a community.

After experiencing, or even hearing, these instances of discrimination, I could imagine anyone emerging from one of the protected classes coming away with hate in their hearts for the dominant culture. I too reflect on stories where my blackness or femaleness was erased. For example, I could not bear to watch John Grisham's *Time to Kill,* where Samuel L Jackson avenges the rape of his adolescent daughter, ravaged so hard by drunken white good ole boys, her little uterus shattered and she would never have children. I remember watching John Singleton's *Rosewood*, where an entire black town in the South was decimated on the cry of "rape" from a white woman. At the time I saw this film, I had a black woman for a boss; she cautioned me about watching such stories before I had to report to work on Monday. Stories of injustice can fill our memories for any group, from holocausts, to internment camps, through the tragic trail of tears.

But many of these stories also include good people, regardless of race or gender, who will stand up and say, "Not on my watch, not with me as a witness you won't." Those souls are the unexpected, the kind, the seemingly invisible, yet they are there and summoned to someone's side when the time comes. Those souls are throughout history; when Dijmon Houson from the *La Amistad* shouted in open court "GIVE US...US FREE! GIVE US...US FREE!" Then President Van Buren blocked the original decision to free the Africans. Shortly after, the former President John Quincy Adams answered the call to defend the Amistad Africans in the Supreme Court appeal. His argument was simple in a time that politicized human civil rights: all men are created equal by definition of the framers of the constitution, that the natural state of man is freedom...*freedom* Any man will try, against all odds, to break forth from his shackles and get home.

As corny as this sounds, I reflect on the character Paula, played by Sandra Bullock in the movie *The Blind Side*. The common response can be, why does the black community need another great white hope? But then let's step further, take race from the lens, see instead the soul of the one being helped, and the soul of the one helping. That lens sees no color. Paula changed Michael Oher's life forever, and perhaps changed the lives of all those her own children would touch as they grew up watching love, fairness and humanity at its best.

So while these thoughts might appear to be a panacea, some universal and ironic white washing of the pain complainant's face, instead it asks the opposite. In the midst of all these stories and interviews, one of the most remarkable stories was a white man who showed the complainant the EEOC and anti-discrimination policies of the organization. This white man led the way, and even filed a similar complaint as he faced adverse action after participating in the internal racial discrimination investigation. He stood up, while a woman of color in the environment refused to participate. See pain and injustice for what it is; continue to fight it on every turn if you can, but remember: the soldiers with you might not have the same hue, but the same heart.

Common mission

Think of all those who faced hoses, dogs, and lynchings. Those who marched so these laws could be on the books, to protect all those covered under Title VII. Perhaps some of us, regardless of race, gender, age, have drifted asleep to the lullaby of affirmative action. Perhaps we thought the fight was over. But the recent EEOC statistics from 2010 show the fight only continues. The rules and tactics of the game have just changed; and it's only half time.

When we use these rules, these laws, we are teaching others — even if one at a time — that it is wrong to treat others unfairly. It is more than unfair to be cavalier and flip about forced separation and adverse employment reaction. We lose our humanity when we ignore the differences and the blessings in diversity. When we harbor hate, and let hate go unchecked, it grows, festers, sticky and stringy against our shoes, like overchewed gum in the tar parking lot on a hot summer day. This cross is not for all to bear, but we all bear the effects of injustice. If you are in a position to fight, the fight has been brought to you because it has been deemed somewhere that you are able to fight it.

Appendixes

Relevant Court Cases, Settlement Information, Commission Information

Selected Court Cases

Hostile Environment Case

SUPREME COURT OF THE UNITED STATES

<hr />

524 U.S. 775

Faragher v. City of Boca Raton

CERTIORARI TO THE UNITED STATES COURT OF APPEALS FOR
THE ELEVENTH CIRCUIT

<hr />

97-282 Argued: March 25, 1998 —- Decided: June 26, 1998

Facts of the Case:

After resigning as a lifeguard, Beth Ann Faragher brought an action against
the City of Boca Raton and her immediate supervisors, alleging that the
supervisors had created a sexually hostile atmosphere by touching, remarking,

and commenting. Faragher asserted that this conduct constituted discrimination in violation of Title VII of the Civil Rights Act of 1964. The District Court concluded that Faragher's supervisors' conduct was sufficiently serious to alter the conditions of her employment and constitute an abusive working environment. The court then held that the city could be held liable. In reversing, the en banc Court of Appeals held that Faragher's supervisors were not acting within the scope of their employment when they engaged in the harassing conduct, that knowledge of the harassment could not be imputed to the City, and that the City could not be held liable for negligence in failing to prevent it.

http://www.oyez.org/cases/1990-1999/1997/1997_97_282

In June 1998, the Supreme Court held that an employer is liable to a sexual harassment plaintiff for an actionable hostile environment created by a supervisor with immediate (or successively higher) authority over the employee. When no tangible employment action results from the harassment, a defending employer may raise an affirmative defense to liability or damages, subject to proof by a preponderance of the evidence. The affirmative defense consists of two elements: (a) the employer must have exercised reasonable care to prevent and correct promptly any sexually harassing behavior, and (b) the plaintiff employee must have unreasonably failed to take advantage of any preventive or corrective opportunities provided by the employer or to avoid harm otherwise. The Court described a "tangible employment action" as including discharge, demotion or undesirable reassignment. Here, the Court held as a matter of law that the City of Boca Raton had not met the elements of the affirmative defense.

As a result of this decision, women who experience sexual harassment at work must find out whether their employer has a sexual harassment policy or other grievance procedure in place. If the employee does not avail herself of the procedures and their protections, she must be prepared to show evidence that her decision was reasonable. Otherwise, she will be precluded from recovering on a claim of sexual harassment.

http://www.equalrights.org/publications/reports/briefing/faragher.asp

Retaliation Case

SUPREME COURT OF THE UNITED STATES

BURLINGTON NORTHERN & SANTA FE RAILWAY CO. *v.* WHITE

CERTIORARI TO THE UNITED STATES COURT OF APPEALS FOR THE SIXTH CIRCUIT

No. 05–259. Argued April 17, 2006—Decided June 22, 2006

Title VII of the Civil Rights Act of 1964 forbids employment discrimination based on "race, color, religion, sex, or national origin," 42 U. S. C. §2000e-2(a), and its anti-retaliation provision forbids "discriminate [ion] against" an employee or job applicant who, *inter alia*, has "made a charge, testified, assisted, or participated in" a Title VII proceeding or investigation, §2000e-3(a). Respondent White, the only woman in her department, operated the forklift at the Tennessee Yard of petitioner Burlington Northern & Santa Fe Railway Co. (Burlington). After she complained, her immediate supervisor was disciplined for sexual harassment, but she was removed from forklift duty to standard track laborer tasks. She filed a complaint with the Equal Employment Opportunity Commission (EEOC), claiming that the reassignment was unlawful gender discrimination and retaliation for her complaint. Subsequently, she was suspended without pay for insubordination. Burlington later found that she had not been insubordinate, reinstated her, and awarded her back pay for the 37 days she was suspended. The suspension led to another EEOC retaliation charge. After exhausting her administrative remedies, White filed an action against Burlington in federal court claiming, as relevant here, that Burlington's actions in changing her job responsibilities and suspending her for 37 days amounted to unlawful retaliation under Title VII. A jury awarded her compensatory damages. In affirming, the Sixth Circuit applied the same standard for retaliation that it applies to a substantive discrimination offense, holding that a retaliation plaintiff must show an "adverse employment action," defined as a "materially adverse change in the terms and conditions" of employment. The Circuits have come to different conclusions about whether the challenged action has to be employment or workplace related and about how harmful that action must be to constitute retaliation. http://caselaw.lp.findlaw.com/scripts/getcase.pl?court=US&vol=000&invol= 05-259

Retaliation Case

SUPREME COURT OF THE UNITED STATES

CBOCS WEST, INC. *v.* HUMPHRIES

CERTIORARI TO THE UNITED STATES COURT OF APPEALS FOR THE SEVENTH CIRCUIT

No. 06–1431.   Argued February 20, 2008—Decided May 27, 2008

In CBOCS West, Inc. v. Humphries, a former Cracker Barrel assistant manager claimed that the restaurant dismissed him because he is African-American, and because he complained to managers that an African-American co-worker was also fired for race-based reasons. The Court held that a longstanding federal civil rights law — first enacted just after the Civil War — "encompasses a complaint of retaliation against a person who has complained about a violation of another person's contract-related right."

The Court held that CBOCS did indeed violate Title VII of the Civil Rights Act of 1964 and U.S.C. §1981 which provides that "[a]ll citizens…shall have the same right…as is enjoyed by white citizens…to inherit, purchase, lease, sell, hold, and convey real and personal property".[1] The court relied heavily on *stare decisis* in its decision, citing *Sullivan v. Little Hunting Park, Inc.* and *Jackson v. Birmingham Board of Education.*

Humphries, an African-American male, sued CBOCS West alleging discrimination and retaliatory firing in violation of Title VII and 42 U.S.C.

§ 1981, based on his discharge as an associate manager at one of CBOCS's Cracker Barrel restaurants. The district court dismissed Humphries's Title VII claims as procedurally barred. It then granted summary judgment in favor of CBOCS West on the § 1981 claim, holding that Humphries could not prove his prima facie case, which requires showing that a similarly situated individual in a non-protected class was treated more favorably than he.

The Seventh Circuit Court of Appeals reversed. First, the Seventh Circuit held that § 1981, as amended by the Civil Rights Act of 1991, applies to claims of retaliatory discharge. Second, the Seventh Circuit found that Humphries had presented sufficient evidence that similarly situated individuals who did not complain about discrimination were not fired.

Age Discrimination Case

SUPREME COURT OF THE UNITED STATES

GOMEZ-PEREZ v. POTTER, POSTMASTER GENERAL

CERTIORARI TO THE UNITED STATES COURT OF APPEALS FOR THE FIRST CIRCUIT

No. 06–1321.   Argued February 19, 2008—Decided May 27, 2008

In Gomez-Perez v. Potter, a postal worker was subjected to various forms of on-the-job retaliation after claiming that her employer violated federal age discrimination laws. The Court held that relevant provisions of the Age Discrimination in Employment Act of 1967 prohibit employers from retaliating against a federal employee who complains of age discrimination.

Petitioner, a 45-year-old postal worker, filed suit claiming that her employer had violated the federal-sector provision of the Age Discrimination in Employment Act of 1967 (ADEA), 29 U. S. C. §633a(a)—which requires that "[a]ll personnel actions affecting employees...at least 40 years of age...

be made free from any discrimination based on age"—by subjecting her to various forms of retaliation after she filed an administrative ADEA complaint. The District Court granted respondent summary judgment. The First Circuit affirmed on the ground that §633a(a)'s prohibition of "discrimination based on age" does not cover retaliation.

http://www.law.cornell.edu/supct/html/06-1321.ZS.html

Shireen A. Walsh, Appellee, v. National Computer Systems, Inc., a Minnesota Corporation, Appellant. Trial Lawyers for Public Justice, P.C.; Program on Gender, Work & Family, Amici on Behalf of Appellee,, 332 F.3d 1150 (8th Cir. 2003)

Federal Circuits, 8th Cir. (23 June 2003)

Docket number: 02-2242

http://vlex.com/vid/shireen-walsh-computer-lawyers-gender-18522815#ixzz0xBRsPWKU

National Computer Systems, Inc. (NCS) appeals from a judgment of the district court awarding Shireen A. Walsh compensatory damages, punitive damages, prejudgment interest, attorneys' fees, and costs totaling $625,526. It argues the judgment should be set aside because all of Walsh's claims are barred by the applicable statute of limitations, and fail as a matter of law because there is no evidence to support the view that Walsh was discriminated against because of her pregnancy under either Title VII or the Minnesota Human Rights Act (MHRA). It further argues that Walsh was not entitled to punitive damages because she did not prove malice or reckless indifference to her rights. Finally, NCS contends that if punitive damages were appropriately assessed, they were excessive. We affirm.

Read more: http://vlex.com/vid/shireen-walsh-computer-lawyers-gender-18522815#ixzz0xBQlEdy1

Business Necessity and Disparate Treatment Case

U.S. SUPREME COURT

GRIGGS v. DUKE POWER CO., 401 U.S. 424 (1971)

401 U.S. 424

GRIGGS ET AL. v. DUKE POWER CO. CERTIORARI TO THE UNITED STATES COURT OF APPEALS FOR THE FOURTH CIRCUIT No. 124. Argued December 14, 1970

Decided March 8, 1971

In 1971, a unanimous Supreme Court issued its opinion in the case of Griggs v. Duke Power Co.,1 holding that for purposes of hiring and assignment to laborer positions, an employer's use of a high school diploma requirement and two standardized written tests, each of which disqualified a higher percentage of blacks than whites, violated Title VII of the Civil Rights Act of 1964.2 The Court stated that it was the intent of Congress to prohibit "...artificial, arbitrary, and unnecessary barriers to employment when the barriers operate invidiously to discriminate on the basis of racial or other impermissible classification."3 Announcing "business necessity" as the legal yardstick for assessing the legality of such standards, the Court held that if an employment practice that operated to exclude blacks could not be shown to be related to job performance, the practice was prohibited. Other than later stating that "any given requirement must have a manifest relationship to the employment in question,"4 the Court did not provide additional guidance regarding the meaning of the phrase "business necessity."

In the 24 years since the Griggs decision, employers and courts have attempted to define business necessity and use it to evaluate a wide range of employment practices. Although the body of law that resulted is complex and difficult for law enforcement managers to apply, certain factors have emerged as keys to assessing the legality of employment practices that create disparity. The factors include:

1. The degree of disparity created by use of the standard
2. The demonstrated factual relationship between achieving the employment standard and successful performance of the job in question
3. Whether achievement of the employment standard is determined by a "neutral" entity external to the employer
4. Whether the employment standard focuses on innate, unalterable characteristics of candidates
5. Whether the job in question has a direct impact on public safety, and
6. The availability of effective alternative standards that create a lesser disparity.

Law enforcement managers have a wide range of employment standards from which to choose. Their departments will benefit if managers choose standards that, in addition to being effective, are on the "good" side of as many of the factors discussed as possible.

For example, because policing involves both decision-making and effective interpersonal communication, frequently with persons of different cultures, mental development and emotional maturity are essential qualities in police officers. In selecting a standard to identify candidates who possess these qualities, a manager might weigh the creation of written tests on one hand versus the use of structured educational requirements on the other. If the effectiveness of the two standards and the disparity created by their use are equal, the factors would favor using the educational requirements because educational achievement is determined by "neutral" entities external to the police department.

http://www.lectlaw.com/files/emp35.htm

Negro employees at respondent's generating plant brought this action, pursuant to Title VII of the Civil Rights Act of 1964, challenging respondent's requirement of a high school diploma or passing of intelligence tests as a condition of employment in or transfer to jobs at the plant. These requirements were not directed at or intended to measure ability to learn to perform a particular job or category of jobs. While 703 (a) of the Act makes it an unlawful employment practice for an employer to limit, segregate, or classify employees to deprive them of employment opportunities or adversely to affect their status because of race, color, religion, sex, or national origin, 703 (h) authorizes the use of any professionally developed ability test, provided that it is not designed, intended, or used to discriminate. The District Court found that respondent's former policy of racial discrimination had ended, and that Title VII, being prospective only, did not reach the prior inequities. The Court of Appeals reversed in part, rejecting the holding that residual discrimination arising from prior practices was insulated from remedial action, but agreed with the lower court that there was no showing of discriminatory purpose in the adoption of the diploma and test requirements. It held that, absent such discriminatory purpose, use of the requirements was permitted, and rejected the claim that because a disproportionate number of Negroes was rendered ineligible for promotion, transfer, or employment, the requirements were unlawful unless shown to be job related

http://caselaw.lp.findlaw.com/scripts/getcase.pl?
court=us&vol=401&invol=424
Regarding Punitive Damages

Legal Rationale for Diversity Training

SUPREME COURT OF THE UNITED STATES

No. 98—208

CAROLE KOLSTAD, PETITIONER *v.* AMERICAN
DENTAL ASSOCIATION

ON WRIT OF CERTIORARI TO THE UNITED STATES COURT OF
APPEALS FOR THE DISTRICT OF COLUMBIA CIRCUIT

[June 22, 1999]

Title VII allows for an award of punitive damages if the defendant committed illegal discrimination "with malice or with reckless indifference to the federally protected rights of an aggrieved individual." 42 U.S.C. 1981a(b)(1). "Reckless indifference" means that the defendant had "knowledge that it may be acting in violation of federal law." Kolstad v. American Dental Ass'n, 527 U.S. 526, 535, 119 S.Ct. 2118, 144 L.Ed.2d 494 (1999). Reckless indifference may be imputed to the employer if an employee commits a discriminatory act while serving in a managerial capacity and acts within the scope of employment. Id. at 543, 119 S.Ct. 2118. We have upheld punitive damages awards in cases where the employer has deliberately turned a deaf ear to discriminatory conduct. Beard v. Flying J, Inc., 266 F.3d 792, 804 (8th Cir.2001) (punitive damages appropriate where specific complaints about sexual assault were made and the company failed to take action); Henderson v. Simmons Foods, Inc., 217 F.3d 612, 619 (8th Cir.2000) (punitive damages appropriate where plaintiff had specifically complained to her supervisors over forty times of sexual assault and supervisors did not take action, refused her request for a transfer).

Read more: http://vlex.com/vid/shireen-walsh-computer-lawyers-gender-18522815#ixzz0xBSfVxBF

About Human Rights Agencies/Human Relations Commission/Human Rights Commission

About Human Rights Agencies AKA Human Relations Commissions AKA Human Rights Commission

Agencies have varying names, often using the words "Human Rights" or "Human Relations" in the name; but there are no standard naming conventions for state agencies across the country. Some states only have an EEOC offices, other states have a human rights or human relationship commission which handles dual filing (with the commission and EEOC simultaneously). Other places have city specific commissions. The length of time to file varies state by state. Some are 180 days; others are 300 days; others are 365 days. Be clear on the laws in the state where the incident occurred (not where the complainant lives). In any case, the complainant does not PAY for the forms or to do an intake session with the EEOC or a Commission. The forms are available on the Internet. Also the number of employees in an organization required will differ. To fall under EEOC guidelines. In some states the minimum is 15 employees, in other states the minimum is 8 employees.

State of Florida

Who Can File?

It is against the law to discriminate in employment on the basis of race, color, religion, sex, national origin, age, disability, marital status or sexual orientation.

An employee or applicant for employment may file complaint when:

- The alleged discriminatory act occurred within the last 365 days
- An employer or potential employer has 15 or more employees
- There is no federal or local agency responsible for accepting alleged complaints of discrimination.

http://fchr.state.fl.us/complaints__1/employment

Commonwealth of Pennsylvania

In general, the law prohibits discrimination based on race; color; religious creed; ancestry; age (40 and over); sex; national origin; familial status (only in housing); handicap or disability and the use, handling or training of support or guide animals for disability. Retaliation for filing a complaint, opposing unlawful behavior or assisting investigations is also illegal.

http://www.portal.state.pa.us/portal/server.pt/community/about_us/18975

State of Washington

All inhabitants of Washington have certain rights and responsibilities under the Law Against Discrimination (RCW 49.60). Under the law, everyone has the right to be free from discrimination at work, in housing, in a public accommodation, or when seeking credit and insurance. Discrimination occurs whenever we treat someone differently and deny him or her equal treatment or access because of: Race, Creed, Color, National Origin, Sex, Marital Status, Family with Children Status, Age, the Presence of any Sensory, Mental, or Physical Disability, the Use of a Trained Dog Guide or Service Animal by a Person with a Disability, honorably discharged veteran or military status or Sexual Orientation/Gender Identity. If you believe you are being discriminated against, try to document what is happening. Keep notes of the dates, times, words used, and actions or conduct you believe is discriminatory. Keep copies of any relevant letters, answering machine messages, etc. Note any witnesses to the action or situation. You have a responsibility to act in a timely manner. Under the Law Against Discrimination, you must file a formal complaint with the Commission within six months of the alleged discriminatory incident or action for employment cases, or twelve months for housing cases.

http://www.hum.wa.gov/ComplaintProcess/Index.html

City of Chicago

Chicago's Commission investigates discrimination complaints, then if there is substantial evidence of a violation, the Commission conducts an administrative hearing and issues a ruling, which may impose fines, damages, and injunctive relief if a violation was proved. The Commission implements the Hate Crimes Ordinance by monitoring hate crimes in Chicago and aiding victims.

Persons who feel they have been discriminated against in Chicago because of membership in one or more of the following 14 "protected classes" may file a complaint with the Commission:

Race	Ancestry
Sex	Sexual Orientation
Color	Gender Identity
Age	Marital Status
Religion	Parental Status
Disability (Mental or Physical)	Military Discharge Status
National Origin	Source of Income

A complaint must be filed within 180 days of the alleged discrimination. Prevailing complainants may receive out-of-pocket damages, emotional distress damages, attorney's fees and costs, and in some cases, punitive damages. A respondent found liable must also pay a fine to the City. http://www.cityofchicago.org/city/en/depts/cchr.html

EEOC Case Settlements

EEOC Cases settled

The following are sample cases compiled directly from the EEOC website. http://www.eeoc.gov/eeoc/newsroom

PRESS RELEASE

MERRILL LYNCH TO PAY $1.55 MILLION FOR JOB BIAS AGAINST IRANIAN MUSLIM FORMER EMPLOYEE

EEOC Settles Suit for Discrimination Based on Religion and National Origin

NEW YORK – The U.S. Equal Employment Opportunity Commission (EEOC) today announced that Merrill Lynch, the international financial services firm, has agreed to pay $1,550,000 to settle a discrimination lawsuit under Title VII of the Civil Rights Act on behalf of an Iranian Muslim former worker who was fired due to his religion and national origin.

The EEOC's lawsuit, in the U.S. District Court for the Southern District of New York (Case No. 07-CV-6017), alleged that Merrill Lynch refused to promote and terminated Majid Borumand from a position as a quantitative analyst in August 2005 because of his Iranian national origin and Muslim religion. Merrill Lynch instead retained and promoted a less qualified individual, the EEOC asserted in the lawsuit.

"Employers need to be vigilant in guarding against discrimination based on religion or national origin, especially as our nation's labor force becomes increasingly more diverse," said EEOC New York District Director Spencer H. Lewis. "All individuals deserve the freedom to compete on a fair and level playing field, which did not occur in this case."

According to the consent decree settling the litigation, in addition to the monetary relief for Borumand, Merrill Lynch will provide training to its employees regarding discrimination based on religion and national origin. In addition, the decree states that Merrill Lynch will not discriminate against employees because of their national origin or religion, and will not retaliate against employees who oppose discrimination. The decree also calls for monitoring by the EEOC to ensure compliance.

EEOC Senior Trial Attorney Michael J. O'Brien said, "We are pleased with the resolution of this case, not only in terms of the significant monetary benefits, but also for the injunctive relief which will help foster a discrimination-free workplace."

The EEOC enforces federal laws prohibiting employment discrimination. Further information about the EEOC is available on its web site at www.eeoc.gov. http://www.eeoc.gov/eeoc/newsroom/release/12-31-08a.cfm

---

PRESS RELEASE

7-13-09

RESCOM SERVICES TO PAY $115,000 TO SETTLE EEOC "MAY DAY" NATIONAL ORIGIN DISCRIMINATION SUIT

Property Service Company Disciplined a Group of Latino Employees, Falsely Assuming They Attended Immigration Rally, Federal Agency Charged

SAN DIEGO, Calif. – ResCom Services, Inc., a Vista, Calif.-based property service company, will pay $115,000 and furnish other relief to settle a national origin discrimination lawsuit filed by the U.S. Equal Employment Opportunity Commission (EEOC), the agency announced today. The EEOC had charged that Latino employees were discriminated against when ResCom disciplined them for being absent from work on May 1, 2006, the day of a "May Day" immigration rally.

The EEOC filed suit after investigating a discrimination charge filed by Latino employee Elvis Lopez, who was suspended from ResCom's San Diego facility after his supervisor assumed he had missed work to attend the immigration rally. In addition to Lopez, the EEOC identified two additional current and former Latino employees who were also disciplined, one even being terminated, for their absence on the day of the rally when ResCom subjected them to false assumptions based on stereotypes shaped by their national origin. ResCom had previously established a policy prohibiting its majority Latino workforce from attending the rally. All three employees had either received pre-approval for their absence or had notified a supervisor in advance of their absences, none of which were related to the rally.

National origin discrimination violates Title VII of the Civil Rights Act of 1964. The EEOC filed suit after first attempting to reach a voluntary settlement.

In addition to the $115,000 in monetary relief, a three-year consent decree settling the suit will also ensure that (1) employees receive annual training regarding national origin discrimination; (2) ResCom will closely track any future complaints to conform to its obligations under Title VII; and (3) the company will provide annual reports to the EEOC regarding its employment practices.

"The days when employers make decisions based on stereotypes and assumptions shaped by the race and national origin of their employees should be far behind us," said Anna Park, the regional attorney for the EEOC's Los Angeles District Office.

Thomas McCammon, the EEOC's San Diego local director, added, "Managers working with employees from diverse backgrounds are at the forefront of bridging the gaps that divide us. The Commission remains committed to working with employers to succeed in this shared goal."

The EEOC enforces federal laws prohibiting employment discrimination. Further information about the EEOC is available on the agency's web site at www.eeoc.gov.

http://www.eeoc.gov/eeoc/newsroom/release/7-13-09.cfm

PRESS RELEASE
4-14-09

SKILLED HEALTHCARE GROUP, INC. TO PAY UP TO $450,000 FOR NATIONAL ORIGIN DISCRIMINATION

Nursing Home Companies Imposed English-Only Rule on Spanish Speakers While Permitting Other Foreign Languages in Workplace, EEOC Alleged

LOS ANGELES – Skilled Healthcare Group, Inc., Skilled Healthcare, LLC, and other affiliated companies, will pay up to $450,000 and provide significant remedial relief to a class of Hispanic employees at its nursing homes and assisted living facilities who were subject to harassment, different terms and conditions of employment, promotion, compensation, and treatment through the implementation of an English-only rule that was only enforced against Hispanics, the U.S. Equal Employment Opportunity Commission (EEOC) announced today.

The EEOC filed suit in 2005 against the defendant companies alleging national origin discrimination on behalf of Hispanics under Title VII of the Civil Rights Act in the U.S. District Court for the Central District of California, which approved the three-year consent decree settling the matter.

"As our country's workforce becomes increasingly diverse, employers must be vigilant in ensuring that if English-only rules are necessary, they are not discriminatory," said EEOC Acting Chairman Stuart J. Ishimaru.

"National origin discrimination is an abomination to our country, which was founded by immigrants and has prospered from welcoming immigrants."

The lawsuit arose from a charge of discrimination by a monolingual janitor, Jose Zazueta, who was fired from defendants' Royal wood Care Center in Torrance, Calif., for violating the company's English-only policy. By contrast, other employees at defendants' facilities who spoke Tagalog were not disciplined or terminated for speaking that language at work.

The EEOC identified a total of 53 current and former Hispanic employees at facilities in California and Texas who were subjected to disparate treatment and harassment based on their national origin and shared Spanish language. The EEOC alleged that some workers were prohibited from speaking Spanish to Spanish-speaking residents of the facility, or disciplined for speaking Spanish in the parking lot while on breaks. Additionally, the EEOC alleged that defendants gave Hispanic employees less desirable work than non-Hispanic counterparts, paid them less, and promoted them less often.

"The EEOC commends Skilled Healthcare for cooperating with us to establish meaningful mechanisms to advance equal employment opportunities for all workers," said EEOC Los Angeles Regional Attorney Anna Park. "In the most diverse state in the nation, employers should not single out certain languages or cultures for harsher treatment."

As part of the, monetary relief for class members, the consent decree provides for the employers to offer English language classes to the 53 claimants. The three-year consent decree also requires that employees receive annual training regarding national origin discrimination; that defendants educate facility residents and patients regarding the rights of the employees under Title VII; that defendants designate an EEO monitor so that future discrimination complaints are closely monitored; and that defendants report annually to the EEOC regarding their employment practices.

EEOC's Los Angeles District Director Olophius Perry added, "Employees and applicants should never be discriminated against because of their language or country of origin. To single out one language but not another for harsher treatment is old-fashioned discrimination."

According to its web site, Skilled Health Care Group, Inc. operates skilled nursing facilities, assisted living facilities, and other facilities totaling 10,100 licensed beds in California, Texas, Kansas, Missouri, New Mexico, and Nevada, mostly in large urban or suburban markets.

In Fiscal Year 2008, national origin discrimination charge filings with EEOC offices nationwide increased to a record high 10,601, up 13% from the prior year. Of the total national origin cases, 204 involved English-only rules, up from 125 such cases in FY 2006 and 32 cases in FY 1996.

The EEOC enforces federal laws prohibiting employment discrimination. Further information about the EEOC is available on its web site at www.eeoc.gov. http://www.eeoc.gov/eeoc/newsroom/release/4-14-09.cfm

---

PRESS RELEASE
4-29-09

MEDICAL WEIGHT LOSS CLINIC TO PAY $68,000 TO SETTLE EEOC DISABILITY DISCRIMINATION SUIT

Weight Loss Chain Fired Employee Over Bipolar Disorder, Federal Agency Charged

DETROIT – A Southfield, Mich.-based chain of weight loss clinics will pay $68,000 to settle a disability discrimination lawsuit brought by U.S. Equal Employment Opportunity Commission (EEOC), the agency announced today. The EEOC had charged that Medical Weight Loss Clinic, Inc. unlawfully fired an employee with bipolar disorder because it regarded her as disabled, even though she had a superior work record with the company.

According to the EEOC's lawsuit (Case No. 2:07-cv-15394 in U.S. District Court for the Eastern District of Michigan), employee Catherine Jovic was a successful employee for more than seven years with Medical Weight Loss Clinic, but was discharged after it learned that she was on leave due to her disability. Such alleged conduct violates the Americans With Disabilities Act (ADA).

As part of the consent decree resolving the suit (entered by Judge

Marianne O. Battani), Medical Weight Loss Clinic will pay $68,000 to Jovic. Medical Weight Loss Clinic also agreed to draft and implement disability discrimination policy training to all of its employees on the ADA.

"We are pleased with the relief provided by the consent decree," said Dale Price, the EEOC attorney who handled the case. "It provides meaningful relief to Ms. Jovic and protections for the employees of Medical Weight Loss Clinic. It also reminds employers that they cannot make employment decisions based on fears and stereotypes about people with various conditions."

The EEOC enforces federal laws prohibiting employment discrimination. Further information about the EEOC is available on the agency's web site at www.eeoc.gov.
http://www.eeoc.gov/eeoc/newsroom/release/4-29-09.cfm

PRESS RELEASE
1-22-09

PITT OHIO AGREES TO PAY $2.43 MILLION TO SETTLE EEOC DISCRIMINATION LAWSUIT

Trucking Company Refused Class of Women Driver and Dockworker Jobs, Federal Agency Charged

CLEVELAND – An interstate trucking firm has agreed to pay $2.43 million and provide other remedial relief to a class of women to settle a major sex discrimination lawsuit brought by the U.S. Equal Employment Opportunity Commission (EEOC), the federal agency announced today.

The EEOC had charged in the litigation that Pitt Ohio Express Inc. denied a class of qualified female applicants, employment as truck drivers or dockworkers since 1997, while men were placed in these positions during the same period.

The comprehensive relief obtained by the EEOC includes $2.43 million for the class of women denied employment. Non-monetary relief includes offers of employment to women who should have been previously hired as drivers and dock workers and equal employment opportunity training to all supervisors and managers, as well as reporting and monitoring provisions.

"We are pleased that this settlement will provide appropriate relief for the people who have been harmed," said EEOC Acting Regional Attorney Debra Lawrence. "We are likewise glad that this employer is taking proactive measures to ensure a discrimination-free workplace in the future by addressing the problems that led to the lawsuit."

The consent decree settling the suit was approved by the court following a fairness hearing held this morning.

According to company information, Pitt-Ohio Express Inc. is a regional carrier specializing in short-haul transporting, providing direct service to over seven states in the northeastern United States. The company is headquartered in Pittsburgh and has terminals in Cleveland, Columbus, Cincinnati and Toledo.

The EEOC is responsible for enforcing federal laws prohibiting employment discrimination based on race, color, religion, sex, national origin, age, disability, and retaliation. Further information about the EEOC is available on its web site at www.eeoc.gov

http://www.eeoc.gov/eeoc/newsroom/release/1-22-09.cfm

PRESS RELEASE
8-21-09

RAMPANT SEX HARASSMENT COSTS LOWE'S $1.7 MILLION IN SETTLEMENT OF EEOC LAWSUIT

Home Improvement Giant Subjected Young Workers to Physical and Verbal Abuse, Retaliation

SEATTLE – The U.S. Equal Employment Opportunity Commission (EEOC) today announced a major settlement of a discrimination lawsuit under Title VII of the Civil Rights Act against Lowe's Home Improvement Warehouse, Inc.

for $1.72 million and significant remedial relief on behalf of three employees in their twenties who were subjected to a pervasive sexually hostile work environment and retaliated against for complaining about it.

The former employees, two young men and one woman, were subjected to widespread and repeated sexual harassment by male and female managers and coworkers at a Lowe's store in Longview, Wash., according to the EEOC. The sexually hostile workplace, which endured for more than six months, included physical and verbal abuse which culminated in one instance of sexual assault.

Among the many allegations in the litigation (Civ. No. CV08-331 JCC in U.S. District Court for the Western District of Washington), the EEOC said the female employee, age 21 at the time, was sexually assaulted by the 44-year-old male store manager in his office. Prior to the alleged assault, the EEOC said she was implicitly propositioned for sex by the manager related to a recent promotion she received. EEOC asserted that Lowe's not only failed to take prompt remedial action to stop the sexual harassment, but also fired the three victims in the case.

"Corporate America should be on notice that sexual harassment and retaliation will not be tolerated by the EEOC," said Commission Acting Chairman Stuart J. Ishimaru. "In this case, severe sex-based harassment of young workers was permitted to run rampant at one of the nation's largest retailers. It is shocking that Lowe's store managers actively engaged in, and even encouraged, such blatant unlawful conduct and then retaliated against the victims for objecting to it."

In addition to the $1,720,000 in monetary relief for the three victims, the three-year consent decree resolving the case requires Lowe's to provide comprehensive training to management, non-management, and human resources employees in all Washington and Oregon stores. Employees will be trained on what constitutes harassment and retaliation, and on their obligation not to harass or retaliate against any individual. Managers and supervisors will be trained on what constitutes harassment and retaliation, their obligation to provide a discrimination-free work environment, and their responsibilities if an employee complains about harassment or retaliation, or if they observe it. Human resources personnel will be trained on what constitutes harassment and retaliation, how to institute policies and practices to correct past discrimination and prevent future occurrences, informing complainants about the outcome of internal investigations, and the steps Lowe's will take to assure a discrimination-free workplace in the future.

EEOC Regional Attorney William R. Tamayo of the San Francisco District Office, which oversees Washington and Oregon, said, "Through this consent decree, Lowe's is demonstrating its commitment to preventing sexual harassment and retaliation going forward, particularly at its 50 stores in Washington and Oregon. No worker, regardless of gender or other discriminatory factors, should ever have to endure harassment in order to earn a paycheck."

In addition to the comprehensive training and monetary relief, the consent decree requires Lowe's to revise its sexual harassment and anti-retaliation policies, issue an anti-harassment statement to all employees in Washington and Oregon, revise its method for tracking employee complaints of harassment, and report regularly to the EEOC on harassment and retaliation complaints which arise in Washington and Oregon stores during the term of the decree.

EEOC San Francisco District Director Michael Baldonado, noted, "The EEOC litigates in the public interest when employers fail to voluntarily comply with the law. It is in the best interest of all employers to have effective anti-discrimination policies and procedures in place to promptly address workplace disputes."

The EEOC consent decree covers 37 Lowe's stores in Washington and 13 stores in Oregon. Cindy O'Hara, a senior trial attorney at the EEOC's San Francisco District Office, led the federal government's litigation efforts. Seattle private attorney Scott Blankenship intervened in the case on behalf of the three victims and served as co-lead counsel with the EEOC.

With headquarters in Mooresville, N.C., Lowe's, a Fortune 500 company, is the second largest home improvement retailer worldwide, operating 1,525 stores throughout the United States and Canada, according to company information.

The EEOC enforces federal laws prohibiting employment discrimination. Further information about the EEOC is available on its web site at www.eeoc.gov. http://www.eeoc.gov/eeoc/newsroom/release/8-21-09.cfm

---

PRESS RELEASE
3-31-09

BRITTHAVEN TO PAY $300,000 TO SETTLE PREGNANCY DISCRIMINATION SUIT

GREENSBORO, N.C. – Britthaven, Inc., a Kinston, N.C.-based nursing home and assisted living chain, will pay $300,000 to settle a pregnancy discrimination lawsuit brought by the U.S. Equal Employment Opportunity Commission (EEOC), the agency announced today.

The EEOC had charged that Britthaven had, since at least 2002, subjected pregnant employees to different terms and conditions of employment than its non-pregnant employees. Specifically, the EEOC said that upon learning that an employee was pregnant, the company required her to obtain full medical clearance in order to continue working. As a result of this practice, Katherine Hance and other pregnant women were forced to take medical leave or were terminated despite the fact that they were fully capable of performing their job duties. Hance worked at the Carolina Commons facility in Greensboro. In addition to the Carolina Commons facility, Britthaven operates 53 other nursing and assisted living facilities in North Carolina, Virginia and Kentucky.

"Working women who chose to have children, should not be penalized or treated differently than other employees simply because they are pregnant," said Lynette A. Barnes, regional attorney for the EEOC's Charlotte District Office. "Employers must remember that paternalistic attitudes toward pregnant employees that result in unequal treatment at work violate federal law. The EEOC will continue to vigorously enforce workplace civil rights laws to remedy and eradicate pregnancy discrimination."

In addition to the $300,000 in back pay and compensatory damages that Britthaven will pay, the three-year consent decree resolving the case (EEOC v. Britthaven, Inc., Case No. 1:07CV00408 in U.S. District Court for the Middle District of North Carolina) includes injunctive relief enjoining Britthaven from engaging in pregnancy discrimination or retaliation and requires anti-discrimination training, the posting of a notice about the EEOC, and reports to the EEOC so that the agency can monitor requests for medical clearance made by the company.

The EEOC enforces federal laws prohibiting employment discrimination. Further information about the EEOC is available on the agency's web site at www.eeoc.gov.

http://www.eeoc.gov/eeoc/newsroom/release/3-31-09a.cfm

PRESS RELEASE
9-30-09

TESSCO SETTLES EEOC RACIAL HARASSMENT LAWSUIT

FOR $125,000

White Laborers Harassed by Hispanics on the Job, Federal Agency Charged

DALLAS – Total Electric and Supply Company, doing business as TESSCO, will pay $125,000 to three former employees to settle a racial and national origin harassment lawsuit filed by the U.S. Equal Employment Opportunity Commission (EEOC), the agency announced today. TESSCO is an energy and utility services company headquartered in Midland, Texas.

According to the EEOC's lawsuit (Civil Action No. MO-08-CV-130 in U.S. District Court for the Western District of Texas, Midland-Odessa Division), TESSCO subjected three white, non-Hispanic employees to a hostile environment. The EEOC charged that the men were subjected to name calling and taunting in English and Spanish on the jobsite. They complained about the harassment, but no action was taken.

Race and national origin discrimination violate Title VII of the Civil Rights Act of 1964. The EEOC filed suit after first attempting to reach a voluntary settlement.

"This case is an example of how traditional thoughts of the direction in which discrimination flows must be adapted to the realities of the changing demographics in the workplace," said Robert Canino, regional attorney for the EEOC's Dallas Office. "Here, it was a Hispanic supervisor and co-workers who subjected non-Hispanics to derogatory comments because of their race. Discrimination of this kind typically originates from a position of power, regardless of which group is the one in charge."

The one-year consent decree resolving the suit, signed by U.S. District Court Judge Robert Junell, provides that the company will require human resources staff and division heads at TESSCO, advising them of the requirements and prohibitions of Title VII of the Civil Rights Act of 1964. TESSCO also agreed to establish a 1-800-Hotline under Title VII.

"EEOC is pleased with this settlement," said EEOC Supervisory Trial Attorney Suzanne Anderson. "The safeguards put into place in this consent decree should ensure that supervisors at TESSCO treat all of their employees appropriately and with respect."

The EEOC enforces federal laws prohibiting employment discrimination. Further information about the EEOC is available on the agency's web site at www.eeoc.gov.

http://www.eeoc.gov/eeoc/newsroom/release/9-30-09h.cfm

Afterword

As we celebrate the 25th Anniversary of the Martin Luther King Jr. Holiday, I remain cautiously optimistic and hopeful. The caution stems from the cross section of race and region represented in these pages. Discrimination is alive and well, for any one who sits in the margins of society. Nonetheless, this practice, whether overt or subconscious, hurts our entire community; the optimism is shown through the individuals who triumph in spite of these barriers and disparate treatment.

I remain hopeful that we as a humane community will continue to fight for equality for women, the racially diverse, ethnic and religious minorities and the disabled. When we suppress people from different walks of life, we suppress the valuable contributions they have to offer. We suppress ourselves.

I applaud Dr. Leah Hollis' work to provide this provocative vantage point into the inner workings of discrimination cases. I applaud the women who have lent their stories so others can learn and progress. And again, I remain hopeful that these voices and the voices of those who have dedicated their lives to eradicating discrimination and injustice will be heard. I am hopeful we will continue this social transformation for equal access and opportunity for all.

Jeffrey Holmes
Higher Education Compliance Officer

Index

A

A Better Chance, Inc. 21
ADA (American With Disabilities Act) 42, 48, 58, 69, 160, 161
ADEA (Age Discrimination in Employment Act) 48, 105, 147, 148
Adverse Action 27, 133, 135, 139, 142
Adverse Impact 76
Age Discrimination 48, 105, 147

B

Business Necessity 149

C

Carole Kolstad, Petitioner v. American Dental Association 151-152
CBOCS West Inc, V Humphries 146–147
Choosing Attorney vii, x, 76, 116, 129, 130, 132– 140, 142, 153
Commission on Human Rights 55, 85, 87, 90
Complainant vii, x, 76, 116, 129, 130, 132–140, 142, 153
Cost to Employer 39
Court Costs 124

D

Disparate Treatment 149
Documentation vii, x, 76, 116, 129–140, 142, 153

E

EEOC iii, vi– x, 7, 11, 12, 21, 22, 24, 26, 27, 34–37, 55, 70, 85–90, 126, 129, 133–140, 142, 145, 152–167
EEOC 2009 Statistics viii, ix, 11
EEOC 2010 Statistics ix, 11, 142
Emotional Stress vii, x, 76, 116, 129, 130, 132–140, 142, 153
Employment Attorney vi
Evaluation 94, 116, 118

F

Faragher v. City of Boca Raton 143
Fired, Terminated iii, 33, 36, 39, 72, 88, 123-127, 131, 155, 157, 159, 160

G

W

CPSIA information can be obtained
at www.ICGtesting.com
Printed in the USA
BVHW040956090220
571839BV00015B/662